All T
For Good

Alyn Haskey

Freedom Ministries Media
A Freedom Ministries Publication

Freedom Ministries
PO Box 24
Nottingham
NG3 4LD

First published 1992

Freedom Ministries Media is the publishing imprint of Freedom Ministries.

ISBN 1 874310 00 9

Cover photo by Alan Rothwell, Nottingham
Cover design by John Billingham, Hitchin
Set in Times Roman
Typset by Mike Taylor, Nottingham
Printed and bound by
Cox & Wyman Ltd., Reading

Freedom Ministries is a registered Charity (No. 327526). It aims to promote and support evangelistic ministry, particularly by people who have a disability. Freedom Ministries supports the work of Alyn Haskey and have funded the publication of this book. All proceeds from the sale of this book are returned to the charity to further its aims and objectives.

Contents

ALL THINGS FOR GOOD
ALYN HASKEY

This is a book about the goodness of God and is centred around Romans 8:28. The writer takes a personal look at the question of suffering, relating it to his disability and faith.

The early chapters go into more detail on some of the incidents mentioned in his first book, "Freedom Ride". He talks about this growing awareness of being different, what it felt like to be away from home, bewildered and hopeless. He then tells of his search for meaning against a background of problems, both physical and emotional. Finally he came to put his trust in Jesus Christ.

Over the next few years life changed in many ways, but going to University, while being exciting, brought him face to face with difficulties such as integration and the frustrations of living in a largely able bodied world.

Believing in a God of power and having received some healing, he struggled with the knowledge that God had done so much and yet he was still in a wheelchair. He was called to a Ministry but how could someone so disabled carry out such a calling? Yet he completed his training in spite of doubts and obstacles, and looked forward to becoming a lay worker, but it did not turn out that way.

The later chapters bring the story up to date and feature his battle for recognition, within the church, problems with health and injury. How he came to write his first book, and his attempts despite setbacks to achieve independent living.

Throughout he relates his experiences to his understanding of scripture, touching on issues of healing, weakness, spiritual warfare, and trust. Most of all he looks at the life of Jesus, who knows all about the hard times in our lives.

The account is full of his experiences of God working for good, and though he is aware that there may be more struggles ahead, he is sure that God's love transcends all the problems we will ever face. God will turn sorrow into joy.

Acknowledgments

I wish to acknowledge the help of Ruth Robinson for her patience, wisdom and wit and many others who helped with the writing and many other tasks. I also wish to thank all the people at St. Paul's Church, West Bridgford, who because of an oversight were not acknowledged in "Freedom Ride" (not my fault!). I want to especially pay tribute to the late Tony Evans, who was always a real friend, my friends at Freedom Ministries, and my new friends at St. Andrew's. Most of all I want to thank Jesus for all that He has done, is doing, and will do in my life. May all glory go to Him.

Alyn Haskey. October 1991

If you would be interested in other publications, how you can help, or wish to invite Alyn to speak to your church, group, school, or other organisation, please write to:

Freedom Ministries
P.O. Box 24
NOTTINGHAM
NG3 4LD

ALL THINGS

One of the questions that I'm often asked is: "How can you be a Christian, believe in a God of love, and be in a wheelchair?". It's an important question because we live in a world of pain, where children are abused, where many suffer from starvation or war, where death appears to run riot, taking no notice of age, where many suffer from painful illnesses, and where sometimes it is really hard to believe in a loving God. Yet I believe firmly that God is love, and that He cares for the pain that we go through, and weeps when we weep. I hope to share with you how I came to know a God of love in a world of pain, and to experience the promise that "all things work together for good to those who love God", Romans 8:28.

PART I

QUESTIONS

Why does it rain
When I want to go out
Why should I whisper
When I want to shout
Why don't the answers
Come straight away
Why do I struggle
Each and every day
Is there someone who can answer
The questions in my head
Or will the solutions
Remain unsaid

– ONE –

We have to begin somewhere, so let's begin with a few facts. The first fact is that we cannot escape from pain. I'm very often asked to speak about suffering, and one of the things I say is that if you haven't suffered so far, praise the Lord, but don't think you'll get away with it. We only need to look around us to see that things are going wrong. You just need to walk down the street, watch the television, or read the newspaper. The crisis in Ethiopia recently reached the world, but there were many other crises of similar proportion. There are earthquakes, famines, volcanoes, fires, wars, plagues, increasing violence, and the possibility that at any moment we will all be blown to non-existence. Maybe even by mistake! There are also chemical disasters, motorway pile-ups, and cancer. No, there is no doubt that we live in a world of pain. And if you are feeling depressed at this point, no one could blame you.

The biggest question is why? Why are we in this mess? Who caused it? Sometimes we may feel that we are carrying the blame for something which is in the past. There is evidence that in one sense this is true. I wonder if you ever wake up in the morning and say "Who started this, and why am I involved in it? What's it got to do with me?"

The most frustrating part is that there is no simple answer to that question, at least, not one which will satisfy it. I can't tell you why at the moment of my birth something went wrong, I can't tell you why I had to live in an oxygen tent for a week. I do know that that changed my life, and that I'm still feeling the effects of it. From then I became a person with severe disabilities. Let's get that straight from the beginning, we are often categorised as disabled people, but the truth is that we are people first, who happen to have disabilities. That in itself is a major problem. For the moment it's enough to say that I entered a world of suffering with problems of my own.

When we talk about ultimate causes, there are no easy answers. God, by the very nature of being God, cannot be comprehended fully by the human mind. We are then left in the midst of a world which has the potential to be beautiful, but which equally can be a living hell. Yet there are some answers to why suffering occurs because, like it or not, we, men and women, have been given a prominent position in "creation"[1]. So when we say "How can God allow this?" this is often only half the question. One of the things we have to come to terms with is that we, too, cause suffering, and part of human nature always wants to blame somebody else[2]. For instance in Genesis[3] Adam puts the blame on Eve, and Eve puts the blame on the serpent. Unfortunately for the serpent there was nobody else he could point to. I am not saying that they were wrong, they were deceived. Nevertheless, they ignored the clear instructions God had given them. When we say "Why doesn't God do anything?" we need to ask the same question of ourselves, why don't *we* do something instead of allowing situations that are obviously not right. This failure to live up to our full potential is a major cause of suffering, both to ourselves and to others.

In considering the cause of suffering, another element is

 [1] Gen.1:26-30 [2] Jas.1:2-18 [3] Gen.3:8-14

that as Christians we are not neutral in the spiritual battle which is going on around us. So often you hear the comment "Become a Christian and all your troubles will end". And often you will hear people say "All things work together for good for those who love God". In other words, it's all going to be all right and we can just sit back and enjoy the ride. I don't believe this is quite what Paul meant. The whole purpose of that part of his letter to the Romans was to show that suffering and glory are both part of our Christian life and we need to note which comes first. Yes, ultimately those who belong to God, who love Him, and have been called and chosen by him will receive a share of His Glory; but the cost of glory isn't cheap, you need only to look at the life of Jesus to see that. Ask yourselves this question: "If salvation could have been achieved by any other way but by the cross, wouldn't God have used it?". Why should God have sent Jesus to earth to live amongst us and to die a painful death on a wooden cross unless it was the only way? And if that were true for Jesus, then why should it be any different for us?[4].

I believe that we are called not only to end suffering but, like our master, to experience it first hand[5]. The pattern we have is the life of Jesus: He says "Follow me". When we decide to do that, then we will experience suffering and pain, from others, with others, and from the enemy, who won't like the fact that we have committed our lives. That sounds frightening, but Paul says: "Who can separate us from the love of God?"[6]. He gives a list of potential problems, most of which he experienced during his life, but then affirms the fact that there is nothing in all creation that can separate us from the love of God. We too can know that, despite the fact that until Jesus comes again we live in a world of pain.

[4] Mk.8:34 [5] Jn.16:33 [6] Rom.8:37-39

– TWO –

If we're not depressed by the fact that suffering is a present reality, then we're probably asking the question "OK, but what do we do?". If we can't escape is there any hope? I believe very strongly that if we give in, then there is no hope. There is a world of difference between saying "I'm disabled, and that's it, I'll just sit back and let it happen" and having the view that disability shouldn't be a bar to life. It's very hard to draw the line between acceptance and resignation, but there is a difference. Some people believe that it's fate and can't be changed, and therefore you just grit your teeth and get on with it. To be honest, I felt like that at one time. I believed that God had given me the lot of being a person who is severely disabled, and that my calling was to be pliant, smiling and generally patient. But it was always awkward, as patience isn't one of my natural abilities and being pliant certainly isn't. There was something inside me that said "So, I'm in a wheelchair, so I can't communicate, but surely God doesn't intend me just to sit here passively, surely He has a purpose for my life?"

The problem was that most of the people I asked were not able to answer my questions to my satisfaction. That isn't a criticism of them. In fact, often the most honest answer is "I don't know" and the most annoying is some glib answer such as "It'll all work out for the best". If suffering is a reality then the mystery of how God can use it is just that – a mystery. There aren't any logical or immediate solutions. Yet I have begun to see that God has a way of rewarding our trust in Him, by doing something beautiful, even in the midst of pain; of taking the very deepest tragedy and turning it round to triumph. It's only when we come and ask Him that we can begin to see the possibilities. That's how it was for me. I'd been a Christian for some years. I believed, I trusted God, and knew he worked miracles, but I hadn't actually experienced anything dramatic in the way of healing. My life had changed, but the changes had been changes of circumstances rather than ability. Of course, I don't want to say that getting O and A levels wasn't important, or that doing the Duke of Edinburgh Award wasn't good, but at the age of 21-22, it seemed as if I'd reached the limit, the pinnacle, as if somehow this was it.

The trouble is that when we taste success and experience change, we want more, and even though I was in the Open University (OU) I wasn't happy or satisfied.

Though life was reasonably independent, at least far more than it had been, I found myself up against situations that restricted me. A world in which a wheelchair and the person in it were not accepted as equal. Entry was refused because of fire risk. Transport was costly because I couldn't just jump onto a bus. On arriving at a building I was faced with steps, and the need to be dependant on others for access with all its attendant risks. My desire to be a "normal" person brought me face to face with the reality that I was different. In one sense I know that most people don't ride about in wheelchairs or walk with sticks, but what hurts most is that along with the physical disability is the implied mental disability, as if somehow the two are connected. So what should I do? Retreat, hide behind doors, or go out with a group where there would be less danger? I know for certain now that I couldn't have done any of these. The other alternative was to take risks, confront people, and just cope with their reactions. What a proposition! Was this what life was going to be like for the next 50 years, a constant struggle for recognition and acceptance? Was I going to have to bear this stigma for something that was, after all, not my fault? I hadn't asked to be born with Cerebral Palsy, and for that matter, no one had asked me if I minded. Why had God picked me to live like this and what did he feel about the situation?

These were the kinds of questions that I needed answers to, not glib answers or platitudes, not questions of *why* that could never be answered, but where was God, what was he going to do about my pain, rejection and frustration?

– THREE –

Trying to find answers to questions is often difficult, especially deep questions like "Why people suffer", and the answers often come in a way we don't expect. I say "answers" very loosely, because often they are only guidelines. They just help us to go that bit further, just open our eyes a little to allow us to take a different stance or viewpoint. A number of the answers for me came through one man, though I've no doubt they were from God. I mentioned in my earlier book "Freedom Ride" that at the age of 23 I was thinking about university, and that I'd been approached to take confirmation classes, but I really didn't have a clue what was supposed to happen at these classes. In fact after the initial approach some time passed before there were any developments, then one day David, who was a curate, turned up and informed me that he was going to be taking my confirmation class. In fact "class" is probably the wrong word as there were only two of us! I guess the powers that be had decided that this was the best way to do it. Perhaps it would save embarrassment and other problems.

The first thing David said was "Have you got any questions?". To this day I'm not sure what confirmation classes are supposed to be like. I'm sure ours didn't follow any recognised form, but I'll tell you this, they were good fun, and I'm not sure who did more talking. For the first time I actually met someone who was prepared to sit and listen to the questions and explore them. I learnt some amazing things, and perhaps the most important was that I needed to get to know Jesus better, that was only way I was going to discover answers to the questions. I discovered that Jesus really did care about the pain and frustration that I experienced. I learned that He wanted to work in my life to do something new. I needed to have much broader horizons, but He made it clear that things wouldn't be easy and situations wouldn't change overnight. I began to understand what being a Christian is all about, and it's a very simple secret – you have to follow Him, to give your life into His hands and to trust Him. Jesus never promised an easy life[7]. So many people assume that when you become a Christian your problems end. Jesus never said that, but He promised to be there[8] and I've discovered that even in the deepest pit He is there too, helping us to get out. I don't want to kid you. I didn't learn all these lessons in one go, but I began to see that Jesus cared much more about my situation than I thought he did, and that was important, especially as I was off to university shortly. There I would meet a complete new situation. How would I cope? What if things went wrong? What if my helpers and I didn't get on? What if there were periods of sickness or depression and I got behind with my work? Most of all, how could I cope with being a person with disabilities in what is predominantly an able bodied world. I suppose if I'd really stopped to think about all these things I might have changed my mind. Fortunately I didn't, I was too excited about the possibilities. I did know that for the first time in my life Jesus wasn't just some idea, some historical person that I knew about, who was "out there". He was

 [7] Jn.16:33 [8] Mt.28:20

here, and real, and if I got into trouble He'd be there to help me.

– FOUR –

My time at the University of York was good, and I've shared a lot about that in "Freedom Ride", but going to university as a person with disabilities obviously had difficulties. With good facilities and the best will in the world you can't legislate for attitudes, and you can't expect everyone to be at ease with severe disability. Each day I spent there threw into sharp focus the differences and also my dependence on others. Initially I was a novelty (in the kindest sense) although I wasn't the first student with a disability at York, and that year there were three others. Nevertheless I've learnt that disability awareness has to do with presence. There may be lasting results, for instance ramps and other adaptations, but each generation of students that are disabled are pioneers. When it comes to integration, there might have been students in wheelchairs in previous years, but that experience had gone and it was back to basics. That's a lesson I've learnt over and over again. It's frustrating but true, and you have to remember this was all very new to me.

When I arrived I'd only known my helper Graham for a couple of days, and in one sense it was the two of us against the world! At first we attracted a lot of attention and good will, and I suppose it was a little bit artificial. There were lots of people who wanted to help, and I was really grateful for that as in the first couple of weeks we had an emergency with Graham being ill. For three days I met a lot of new people very quickly, and I'm not talking about socially – that was happening as well. I'm talking about people taking care of my intimate needs. It isn't easy to ask a stranger to take you to the toilet, let alone undress you. Perhaps people think that as it's your lifestyle you're used to it, but it doesn't work like that, and it can be a very awkward situation. My speech at that time wasn't anywhere near as clear as it is today, so there was every possibility of being misheard, misunderstood and for things to go wrong. You're aware that this is an awkward situation, and it places tremendous pressure on the relationship. It may put people off, perhaps permamently, and end any possibility of that relationship developing further. I can remember one student telling me that he just could not cope when he came near me, not because of anything I had done, simply because of the situation I was in. He just couldn't cope with the perceived pain and I suppose if we're honest, few of us can.

The thought of being unable to hear, see, having to live in a wheelchair or be restricted by any other limitation, confronts us with the reality that there is pain and suffering. Reactions to this are various – either we want to run away and have nothing to do with it, or we feel a sense of relief that it isn't us, maybe we feel obligated, but don't really want to give ourselves to the situation or we really do want to understand and to get alongside. I met all kinds of reactions at university, not just to pain but to disability. I had made the assumption that being intelligent, people wouldn't react to my disability in a negative way, they would understand being in a wheelchair didn't make me any less of a person. It doesn't work like that. One of the biggest problems was in forming relationships. Fortunately, Jesus gave me some initially that were really good ones, for instance the Chaplain, and people I met at Church on the first Sunday. But it took time, and there was an assumption that if Graham was there, I was OK and people didn't need to make any effort to come near. After a while we solved this problem. Graham would take me to a place and depart, having arranged a time for collection if all else failed. Of course that was no guarantee, as often the next person I spoke to would be Graham, when he came back.

After the first term things did begin to improve. The sight of the wheelchair (and me) became more accepted. We noticed that the initial enthusiasm of offers to help gradually decreased. At first this was worrying, however those who continued to come became real friends. As I write this, or should I say dictate it, I am aware of something Paul says in his letter to the Phillipians. He rejoiced at how God was using his situation to proclaim the good news[9]. You see, the fact is that I have to depend on people, not just at university, but even today I have to ask people to do things for me, perhaps to write, to make a cup of tea or perform one of my songs, this brings me face to face with my limitation. Yet God's grace is such that most of my closest friends initially came to help me in some way: here is an example. Phil, who is now a vicar, came to sing a song I had written for a service, because he can play a guitar and I can't.

People from church came initially as part of a writing rota, others who weren't Christians came to do things, such as write letters and I was able to share the good news. No one likes to be dependant if it can be avoided, but God can make use of any situation. Is this an example of "All things working for good"? If I really think about it, the Lord has led the right people to me at the right time, be-

 [9] Php 1:12

cause I needed their gifts. They came as volunteers, but many have become lifelong friends. They came maybe in fear or anxiety, not knowing what to say or what to do. However, there have been blessings on both sides – often people say that they have learnt much, just from being with me. I'm not boasting, but I want to share how God can work if we give Him the freedom to do so.

– FIVE –

God was beginning to work in some areas, there were others in which he seemed very far away. Have you ever felt locked in or tied down? Have you ever felt like breaking out of the house and just running? Have you ever felt isolated, knowing that God is there, but somehow still seemingly alone, as if there is no-one to turn to, no-one to understand how you feel at that particular moment? Perhaps you get up, put on a coat and go for a walk. Perhaps you pace the room. All of us have ways of exorcising those feelings. There are a variety of reasons as to why we might feel like that. Maybe we're ill. I can remember at university one period of illness when the symptoms just went on and on. Whatever we tried didn't bring any relief. I was physically not right, and emotionally down in the dumps. Or maybe its a relationship that's not right.

One of the most amazing miracles at University was that in three sets of helpers, that's to say six individuals, we never actually came to blows or had any serious breakdowns, but that didn't mean there weren't tensions or disagreements. It's a very difficult balance to achieve. You are aware that here are people who volunteer to look after you for a year during term time. The local authority are impressing on you the importance of making it work. You want these people to get the best out of the experience, to have enjoyment, to have relaxation. You want to be fair, but there is always the possibility of abuse. This can come in many different ways, from over-familiarity that can lead to rudeness, to exploitation. I have been put down in public many times, in front of friends, by people who should know better, and of course there is just sheer thoughtlessness. I'm sure I won't offend anyone if I say that it happened.

When it did I felt powerless to do anything about it, frustrated as the odds were usually 2-1, and isolated because there was no-one I could turn to. Please don't get me wrong, we didn't have constant battles. They weren't ogres, in fact they were very caring, and I will always remain grateful for all the help they gave me. But in any relationship we don't always live up to expectations. Things go wrong, and there is blame on both sides. I just wanted to give you some idea of the sort of things that happened, some of the feelings I experienced. You see, I couldn't get up and go for a walk, even though I wanted to. I couldn't go off to the sports centre and kick a ball around. What do you do in a wheelchair when you feel angry, hurt, upset, when you feel isolated? There was only one thing I could do really, and that was pray. Well, there was an alternative, I could cry, but in many ways praying was easier, because at that time in my life I didn't want to share my feelings in public. I'd been brought up with the idea that you shouldn't cry in front of people, but should wait until you are on your own and never let people know what you really feel. Behind closed doors, with a stereo playing, and in the presence of Jesus, that's the place to cry, always being careful to wipe my eyes when I'd finished – which is not that easy! As a child I was encouraged not to show my emotions in public. This was reinforced by my father's pronouncement that, "Big boys don't cry!" I grew up with these influences, and, to a lesser degree, they are still there. In Jesus I found someone who would listen, and still does.

It's as I talk to him of my frustrations, anger and pain, that I know that He understands; this doesn't solve all the problems. There were times at university, and since, when I've had to close the doors often and be alone, but usually by the time I've finished I feel better, and I either emerge with a solution, a spirit of forgiveness or just with His strength to keep going until its sorted out. At any time we need to know Jesus is there, ready to listen and to lift us so that we can carry on.

– SIX –

One of the main joys of university is the social life. In fact, it can be a danger unless you exercise discipline. There are so many things you can get into, ranging from sport, to politics, to social welfare, or just having friends. I was determined to make the most of my opportunities. Friends have said that when they were crawling into bed tired they knew that I was probably still involved in something! That very involvement makes you painfully aware of your limitations. I was a very keen supporter of the College football team, watching all the games, writing reports for the sports newspapers and generally regarded as one of the team. I remember a dinner where we all had great fun. They could even accept the fact that I was drinking tomato juice, having given up alcohol for Lent, but of course there was one essential difference. No matter how welcome they made me feel, there was no way I could put on the college football shirt and play. I was faced by that fact every time I watched a game. The same was true for 5-a-side football, where I was the non-playing captain of a side. I could come on for the kick-about, but as soon as the whistle sounded for the game to start, I would have to leave the pitch.

I'm sure there are many of us who are passionate about a sport and want to get into the action but can't. That's not to say I didn't play football. There were friendly games and there were the two memorable occasions when the local PHAB side thrashed both the University and our college. However, I would never be able to represent York at sport, it was always the case that for a lot of activities, all I could do was watch.

Within the Christian Union, and the Chrisitian community, there were many trips. In my first term we went to a monastery. That was my first encounter with silence. I've struggled with it ever since! Being quiet might be a gift, but I don't think its mine. In the afternoon we went for a good brisk walk in the Yorkshire countryside. But there were the usual difficulties – places where you couldn't take a wheelchair, or steps. Sometimes there were barbecues on the beach, followed by games. Everybody likes to run around on the beach, but you can't do that in a wheelchair, the wheels get bogged down. There were services to organise or take part in, and of course there were songs to write. God has given me this gift, which is a real joy, and yet it is a frustration. Imagine a head full of ideas, and not being able to communicate them. Little harmonies that you can't put over; an irregular rhythm that makes the song interesting, but somehow no matter how hard your friends try, they just can't pick it up, not because of their inadequacy, but because music is something you can only demonstrate by playing. Imagine the joy and the frustration of hearing someone singing your song, yet realising you can't contrast the skill of the guitarist against fingers that won't do as they are told. Life is full of limitations, realisation that somehow we can never do all we want to. That can be painful. Yet even in these areas I experienced that Jesus cared and understood, and believed that He would work it out for good.

– SEVEN –

Towards the end of my time at university a crisis arose. Not over faith, body or mind, but rather the future. Jesus had used the time at York to develop a real ministry, in spite of initial doubts, and it wasn't long before I started to get invitations to talk about suffering and faith. How could I relate my disability to a loving God? What had God got to say on the subject? What was he going to do about it? What about healing? In my final year I went to St-Michael-le-Belfry, David Watson's church where I saw and heard all kinds of miracles, such as people being healed and relationships restored. But what of my own situation? At first I found it easier to say I was too busy to go to healing services. That was true, finals year is always busy, especially when you know there are six papers coming up and you're expected to be able to answer some of the questions on each! It wasn't that I was worried. I wasn't saying "God does it for others, why not for me?" – if anything, I was saying the opposite "I'm all right, let other people be healed", and to be honest, that was true. I felt quite happy seeing other people have miracles. I knew that God loved me and that he had already done some incredible things in my life.

It has to be said that the people who are closest to you often bring great pressure with their love and concern, so I found I was constantly being invited to healing services, and having to find reasons not to go, not because I didn't believe, it just wasn't for me. Towards the end of the year I did go to one, but nothing dramatic happened! However, I did begin to realise that God wanted to do more. I mention this experience because it raises the issue of healing, which can be an area of pain if not fully understood.

What do we mean by healing? So often we see an obvious need and feel that's what that person needs prayer for. I believe however there is a difference between having a feeling, and being led by the Holy Spirit, not because we shouldn't pray for that person, but because we need to know what God wants. People often pray for me, and I appreciate it very much. Yet the simple fact is that at this time God chooses that I should remain in a wheelchair. Therefore is a person's prayer that I am instantly healed, the right prayer? When people pray and nothing happens – or should I say nothing tangible happens, it raises all sorts of questions. "Is it my faith that is inadequate or theirs? Is it a question of sin? Is it demon possession – is exorcism needed? (It's been tried). Is it that I'm not really a Christian? There are many reasons why visible healing doesn't always happen. It could be that it's not God's will, and the person who is the object of prayer shouldn't be made to feel guilty, nor should their faith be questioned.

Now I'm not saying this is just a problem between able-bodied people and those with disabilities – we all do it. It's so easy to pray for the most obvious thing when in fact that person's need is far deeper. But if you are in a wheelchair you are perhaps a more obvious target. I can remember at Billy Graham's "Mission Sheffield" having to fight off counsellors. It's also happened at Mission London, the assumption being that I needed to become a

Christian even though I'd given my testimony the day before. It is part of God's grace that I'm able to laugh off situations like that. But the serious point is that God's will is supreme, and far beyond our comprehension. Because when you hold in tension the fact that on one hand God is all powerful and can heal, and on the other that there are a lot of people who apparently haven't been healed then either there is a contradiction or more truly we don't know everything about God.

During this period, I saw God work in many ways, especially through finals. When you rely on your voice for exams because you can't use your hands, and have a cold the whole time then it can only be God's power that gets you through. Incidentally, if I'd taken notice of what was happening then, I might have been more prepared for some of the things that have happened since. For surely here is a clear example. It must have been God's will for me to get through this final hurdle at university, yet at the same time he allowed me to have this problem throughout the whole period, but of course I didn't realise it at the time. It is only in the years since then that I've learnt that God's power is supreme over everything.

Very often we talk about having "hindsight" when we begin to understand what God was doing at a particular time. We might wish that we could have hindsight before things happen but we can't. What I do believe is that the more we know of God through Jesus the more we are able to understand the way he works, and hopefully to put our trust in Him. There have been many times in my life when I have suddenly realised that God was at work in a situation that happened five or ten years ago and that situation is directly related to where I am now.

– EIGHT –

When I left University I didn't know what was going to happen. I had been hoping that I could stay in York, but that didn't come off. The only thing I knew for certain was that I was being called to train for some kind of ministry. But not for at least a year, as it seemed quite clear that I shouldn't go from one course to another. I had the possibility of working with a community theatre group and the hope that once back in Nottingham I could continue my training as a lay-reader helping out at St. Paul's, my home church. I returned to Nottingham with mixed feelings, but I knew enough about Jesus to be obedient. Anyway, long term plans could wait until September. First of all there would be results, then graduation, hopefully; then some summer activities which would include four weeks' outreach at the Ranch Adventure Centre, a christian outdoor pursuit centre, just outside Harlech in Wales. This changed my life.

When the Lord reveals that he wants to do something in our lives we have to be open. Going to the Ranch made that possible. There were still lots of questions. After all, I was severely disabled. How would I fit into a team? What could I do? The year before, it had just been a week with people who were used to me. This would be different. I can remember the night before thinking "Will I cope with this?" The experience of the journey did nothing to lessen my apprehension. The eight hour journey was the longest I had made by myself on a train, up till then, and by four o'clock I was getting a bit fed up. It was hot, I was thirsty and stuck in a railway station in the middle of nowhere. Well, Wales! It's a journey I've made many times since, and it doesn't get any easier, and I suppose looking back it was another pointer of things to come, for since those days British Rail and I have got to know each other very well.

At last I arrived and was met by welcoming people. After a short rest, and a welcome cup of tea, I was pitched straight into the action. It was a couple of days later when things really began to happen. We were having a prayer meeting, something, to be honest, that I wasn't quite at ease with. I enjoyed the choruses, but when it came to prayer my ideas were quite limited. I sat with my eyes shut, and suddenly there were hands on me. I wasn't sure what I was expected to do, so I just sat, eyes closed, and waited, determined not to panic. What came next was a message from the Lord saying he wanted to heal me.

He began almost immediately. Over the next few days, several things happened, physical improvements that I could never have imagined – speech, co-ordination and an addiction to prescribed drugs were all touched by Jesus in a new and powerful way. Every day there was some new miracle, powerful and exciting, so much so that perhaps many of us believed that any day I would get up and walk. By the time I got home I was convinced my days in the wheelchair were numbered. I still believe that. I've learnt a lot of hard lessons because there came a time when suddenly the miracles appeared to stop. I say "appeared to" because we always look for the big signs and forget about the grace that is available to us each day. We need to realise that every day is a miracle. The trouble was, I'd got used to the big signs.

In one sense I was hooked on them just as much as I'd been hooked on drugs before. Measuring progress is exciting; to be able, for example, to say: "This time last year I couldn't do this" is brilliant. However, at the same time I believe that if things had happened too quickly I wouldn't have been able to cope with the changes. It was possible that my whole life could have changed overnight – would I have been ready for that? All I had experienced up to then was life in a wheelchair – how would I cope with being able to walk?

During that Autumn I was faced with several crises. The euphoria of university had worn off. I was back in the hostel with nothing to do most of the time, not many friends around, especially of my own age or interests. I was given the occasional opportunity to participate in ministry at St. Paul's, but at St. Nicholas, my other church, this was quite difficult. It seemed I was back to square one, trying to build up relationships or gain acceptance. The fact that I now had letters after my name didn't seem to make a lot of difference to my lifestyle. I also felt isolated at home, and my work with the community theatre group wasn't all I'd hoped for. Added to this, any healing seemed to come to a standstill. There were nights when I felt isolated and alone, except for the presence of God. There was no news about college, and when the production ended, early in the New Year, nothing to do.

There are times when we feel all we have achieved is insignificant. It's a common feeling especially when you have experienced a spiritual and emotional high point. I have coined a phrase for it – the Elijah syndrome – when you have seen the Lord do really exciting things then you come back to earth with a bump, apparently going nowhere[10]. No-one seems to be in tune with you. When

[10] 1 Ki.19

you feel an outsider. I'm sure that's how Elijah felt the day after Mount Carmel[11]. This faithful servant had stood up for God and a great victory had been won, but to Queen Jezebel it meant nothing, and still Elijah was threatened with death. It's the kind of feeling you get in the guard's van of a train, when you've just spent a weekend in church, telling people what it's like to be disabled. They've begun to understand, and yet here you are the day after, with people still staring at you, and you're thinking "When will people understand?". Elijah must have thought – "When will they turn back to you, Lord?". It isn't easy experiencing pain and doubts, but Jesus is there, and He's the one that makes the anguish worthwhile. He's the one who can say "All right, so you haven't done anything new this week, but no-one can deny what I've done in you, and I've promised to do much more". He's the one who says "Don't worry about the doors being shut, I've got the keys. When I open a door, it stays open, and when I shut it, it stays closed[12]". He's the one who says "You're not really alone, I'm here. No matter how dark the night is, the day is coming. No matter how isolated you feel now, you belong to the family of God". Yes, it was a time of survival, but Jesus is the greatest survivor, death couldn't hold him. Even the longest winter turns into spring.

[11] 1 Ki.19:1-18 [12] Rev.3:7-8 (Author's paraphrase)

– NINE –

No-one should be under any illusion that being a Christian is easy, yet so many are surprised by the problems that arise. I believe that many people interpret the message of Jesus as "believe in me, and you'll be all right". But it isn't like that, and Jesus never said it would be. Like it or not, Christians are soldiers, caught up in a battle that they didn't start and can't avoid[13]. To be a Christian is to make a commitment to Jesus Christ, and the kind of commitment Jesus calls us to is very clear in the scriptures "If anyone follows me, let him take up his cross"[14].

It's taken me many years to get to grips with that call, because I believe now that when Jesus said *his* cross he meant exactly that. It's personal. In other words, the battle that we fight isn't only for Jesus, but it's also about our own lives. The minute we become Christians, we enlist and the enemy knows about every weakness we have. Jesus once gave me a picture of the situation we are in. Imagine a spoilt child playing a game. He loses the game, but won't accept the result, so he continuously grouses and spoils it for everyone else. The plain fact is that when Jesus rose from the dead on the third day he overcame everything that ruins our lives. The trouble is that we have

 [13] Eph.6:12 [14] Lk.9:23 (Author's paraphrase)

an enemy who is like a spoilt brat. He knows he's lost. He knows he can't change the result, but he can make our lives a misery, and if he's really clever he can stop some people finding out what the true result is. Just for the record, the truth is this: Jesus Christ offers everyone the freedom to live the kind of life that God intended we should live. He came to bring us life in abundance, and everything else is second best, and not worth having[15].

There is however a difference between knowing the truth, believing it, and living it. This is the area where the hardest battles are fought. "Is God going to heal you?" Has He really called you to a ministry? Have you truthfully achieved anything with God's power? Will you ever get out of that chair? Can you have a life that's full? These were the kinds of questions that were being asked, along with more specific ones. How about that shoulder? Why doesn't it get better? Perhaps God can't do it. And the cough, it's been prayed for many times – why won't it go away? Can't God stop the pains in my stomach? Will you be able to finish one year at theological college, let alone three? What about the steps, what about keep? Yes, we know you can study, but what of practical training? Can you really be a lay-reader – surely not?

There's a story about a man called Job who was faithful to God[16]. One day, the heavenly powers were gathered together, and God said to Satan, or the accuser, "What about my servant, Job? See how faithful he is". The accuser said "Ah, yes, but that's because you bless him. Take away his blessings, and he'll curse you". So God gave permission for Job to be tested, and in the rest of the book, it tells us how Job comes to terms with that, and how, in the end, he had to accept that God is supreme.

One day, Jesus was passing by a pool[17]. There were lots of people with disabilities around the pool[18], waiting for the water to bubble. The first one in had a chance

[15] Jn.10:10 [16] Job 1 & 42 (Author's precis)
[17] Jn.5:1-2 [18] Jn.5:1-15

of healing. Amongst them there was a man who had been ill for 38 years. Jesus asked him a question "Do you want to get well?". Now I don't know about you, but on the face of it that was not one of the most profound questions, or was it? Did Jesus know more about this man than was obvious? We needn't worry here about the excuse the man gave, or the healing itself, it's the question that is important, because I suddenly realised Jesus was saying to me "Do you want to get well"? and without the Holy Spirit it would have been easy not to hear that question amongst all the other questions that I was dealing with.

Maybe for a lot of us, in times of crisis, we don't hear the right question. If God was going to heal me, I had to be ready for it, whether it was today, tomorrow, or in five years time, and the fact was that I wasn't ready. I was afraid. After all, even though I'd experienced quite a lot of healing, I was still quite comfortable, even though the Lord had said "I'm going to heal you completely", did he really mean that? As I said earlier, there's all the difference between knowing, believing and living. I knew that God wanted to heal me. I believed he could do it, but I wasn't living out that belief, because to live it out means that even if there is no apparent progress, you are still trusting. It means that despite setbacks God will work it out. Many of the battles that we fight have to do with the mind, and I needed to have a change of mind. In fact, I needed to stop living as a disabled person and start living as a person who would eventually lose his disability, and there is a world of difference between the two. I had to allow Jesus to take away the fear of being changed, and to give Him freedom. I wouldn't want to say things changed overnight, nor would I want to pretend that since that day there haven't been problems – there have. If that had happened, this book could end here. But during the early part of 1978 I spent a lot of time with Jesus, and I emerged a different person. By the time summer came, I was preparing for training at St. John's Theological College. I discovered later that many miracles happened. All objections had been overcome, the questions answered, and it was time to move on to the next battle.

PART II

PROMISES

You didn't promise me
Sunshine every day
An important job
Good wages
A comfortable house
A happy marriage
The best car on the market
Holidays on the continent
A sure fire pension
You did promise
To be with me always

– TEN –

Life at St. John's was not easy. There were many obstacles, including a community which had its own problems. I'm never at my best early in the morning, so getting up at 6.30 a.m. or earlier was not something I enjoyed. Added to this was the fear that the transport would not arrive on time. That was just the beginning of the day. Let me explain that although St. John's is very open to people with disabilities having provided a ramp, (albeit steep!) the college is far from ideal. To eat, worship and engage in a few other activities you have to be carried up a flight of steps. Even though the person looking after you might be good at handling a wheelchair, there's no guarantee that the other three will be! We had quite a few near misses, including one when I actually flew through the air! Fortunately I landed back in the chair without too much damage. On another occasion, while practising a sketch for a Christmas party, one of my friends threw my satchel at me. Only when it hit me did he remember that there were quite a few heavy books inside.

During the early part of the second term I noticed something was wrong. I began to get pains in strange places, I went off my food, in fact I could eat very little –

unusual for me, for while I've always been a fussy eater, quantity has never been a problem! Over the next few months I lived off toast with very little else, and the pain was there regularly. Added to this was a mysterious swelling in my ear which though treated with tablets, didn't get any better. I had to miss college to see the doctor. People prayed for me and nothing happened (I've got used to that now!).

I didn't know it, but it was the beginning of a troublesome year – or two! I can't remember actually getting depressed, but I did get fed up. It seemed to be one of those situations which I have become used to, of things taking a long time to sort themselves out. It was only later that God taught me valuable lessons about Himself. That's not to say things didn't improve, they did, but they were replaced by other problems. For instance, the swelling in my ear, after various courses of antibiotics, was finally diagnosed as cauliflower ear. Still to this day I have no idea why, but after the appropriate treatment it cleared up (even if it was a little painful). As for the other problem, the Easter vacation saw the beginning of the resolution of it.

I went off to the Ranch for a rest, some speaking opportunities and to do some writing. It was a conversation with a friend that shed light on the problem. In simple terms, it seemed that my body was reacting to stress, either from college, or life generally. I was prayed for during the week and things improved dramatically. For the first time in ages I was able to eat, or eat anything without pain. There were two important lessons to be learnt. First of all, obedience. It's so important to realize that medical and Christian healing are not in conflict. It isn't a case of believing in one and ruling out the other. I should have gone to the doctor. Now I have to be honest, and say that after the cauliflower ear, I didn't have quite the same trust. In this instance, not going resulted in the return of the pains, until eventually I had no choice. The strange thing is, when I did see a doctor, he prescribed tablets, and I only ever needed two. After a while the problem just disappeared.

The second lesson was that God was telling me to slow down. It is interesting that when the pains came, I stopped, prayed, rested, and things sorted themselves out. That's probably why I didn't need many tablets. So by the summer of 1979 I was coming to the end of my first year – and I'd survived. I still had exams to come, but as long as they were all right I'd be allowed to stay and finish the course. I was beginning to discern God working in a different way, but over the next few months my eyes were really opened, and I began to understand what being a Christian is all about. It was a new stage in my life, and one that if I'd really known about beforehand, I might have asked to be excused. However, God knows far better than we do what we can cope with, and doesn't give us that option. That might seem hard, but I've come to see it as a privilege. What God is saying is that he can trust us to go through it, knowing we will be all right, and even though the situation might be tricky, I'm pleased to follow Him in the hope of bringing glory to His name.

– ELEVEN –

I hope you understand that I'm just picking out certain things. This is not a chronicle of woes. I want to show that the God I believe in is able to turn sorrow to joy. I can do this best by sharing some of the things that have happened, but I want you to remember that they are set against a background of positive things, so it's good to be reminded that after a summer of torture (revision) I did pass my exams. The prize, two more years at St. John's, this time with a full-time helper which eased the load on other students considerably.

During the summer itself there was more healing – my speech seemed to be getting clearer all the time. In September there was a mission in Nottingham, which started off with me wondering if I'd ever get any part in, and ended with me being asked to do things in all directions. I believe quite sincerely that Jesus never promised that everything would be easy. If you really look at his words[19], it's anything but. By nature we want the easy parts, we want the glory without the suffering, the victory without the battle, the prize without the contest. I can remember a time in my life when I really believed that as Christians we inherited everything, nothing was a prob-

 [19] Jn.16.33

lem, and especially that persecution[20] wasn't for us. But it isn't true. Peter wrote to the dispersed Christians, saying "Why are you surprised at the trials you are going through?"[21] Suffering is not unusual. The important thing to know is whether we deserve it. Some things we do naturally bring consequences. For example, if we are professing to be Christian, and yet not living a Christian life, we deserve to be slated. Believe it or not, we're being watched from two directions, by people around us and by the spiritual powers (remember Job!). Peter also says "Make sure that you're not being punished for the wrong things".

There are other factors we've got to take seriously. There are those who don't want to hear the Good News and don't want anything to do with it, and there is also an enemy who is determined to make a misery of our Christian lives. Peter calls him a roaring lion who prowls around ready to devour us[22]. He knows our weaknesses and our faults. He's going to do his best to destroy us, disable us, or at the very least hold us back, and how we react is the key. Remember the conversation between Satan and God about Job. "If you let him get hurt he will curse you and turn away from you". It's easy to be a Christian when everything is going well, when day to day we see God's provision, and when we see miracles in progress. Job had every blessing, but it's when things that we've prayed for don't happen, or when we're ill and we don't get better, what then? I was about to find out and to learn more about God's goodness. My weakness is my body, the enemy knew and was about to test that very severely.

It's bad enough when you get injured, but when its doing the Lord's business, it does tend to raise a question in your mind. It was a typical Ranch night, a barbecue for all those who were staying there that week. For safety reasons it had to be away from the main buildings. I'm

[20] Mk.13: 5-14 [21] 1 Pe.4:12-19 (Author's precis) [22] 1 Pe.5:8-9

pleased to say that they make very few concessions to the fact that I'm in a wheelchair, and that's especially true of the barbecue site. It's enough to say that going on wheels is not the most convenient way of getting there! Therefore, with the measure of healing I had received up to that point we hit on the idea of "walking". Not the most accurate description, as it tended to be part stagger and part drag, with two able assistants, or variations on that figure! On the way down there were no mishaps. Unfortunately on the way back it was getting quite dark, and two of us stumbled. I didn't think anything of it at the time, because I'm used to having a few knocks and bruises. But praise God, I'm also fairly tough. My shoulder ached a little the following day but not enough to really concern me. However, some time after I came home, when I began preparing for college, I noticed the pain seemed to be getting worse. This, added to a persistent cough, made me seek prayer.

I went to friends at church who prayed and assured me that things would soon improve. They didn't, in fact both problems went on well into the new term, when at last the cough disappeared, but any hopes of the pain in my shoulder doing the same soon evaporated. The real problem was that the shoulder needed rest, which was the very thing I was not able to give it, so it became a vicious circle. The pain set off spasms, and the spasms increased the pain. A doctor's prescription gave minor relief. Prayer didn't seem to be achieving anything. I began to look at my life to see if there was some unconfessed sin, but the Holy Spirit didn't point to anything. I wondered if I was out of God's will, but again there was no evidence to suggest that. So why wasn't God healing my shoulder? I couldn't understand it, after all, God heals. I've seen it and experienced it, and surely he didn't want me to go through pain. By Christmas the shoulder was becoming a real nuisance. When the pain came it disrupted everything – work, ministry, pleasure, and relief was getting harder to find.

In early January I was to preach for the first time at St. Paul's, my home church. The pain began at about seven o'clock in the morning, and I can't remember it letting up at all that day, until the miracle. Throughout the day I wondered if I was really in a fit state to preach God's Word, especially with the added tensions of it being my own church, my tutor being there, my sermon class (fellow students, who assess your preaching) and the rector of the parish! But God kept telling me I was the one appointed to proclaim his word. By six o'clock I was physically a wreck, but praise God, I've learnt since then, that proclaiming the Good News has nothing to do with how we feel. All we need to do is put our trust in Jesus, or speak by the power of His Holy spirit. I've still got letters from people who heard me preach that night. They talk about how clearly my voice came over, and how the Holy Spirit touched them, and you know, I don't remember feeling any pain while I spoke. One of the readings that night was Isaiah 43.1-5 where through the prophet God promises to be with us. Whether we walk through fire, or go through water, we will not be harmed. I'd learnt part of the lesson, but there was more to come.

– TWELVE –

Towards the end of the book of Job[23] there is a conversation between God and Job. It's a conversation that asks the basic question – who really is wise? God unfolds before Job the wonders of his creation and asks Job pointedly "Were you there? Do you understand it?" Wisely Job admits that he knows very little, and towards the end of his life God blesses him as richly as he had before. I mention this because God's word is full of those who sought him and asked questions, questions which are so important, such as "Why do the wicked prosper? Why does the sun shine on the righteous and unrighteous" and particularly for Job, why has God allowed him to go through these trials – what is it for?

I believe that part of a mature Christian relationship is being able to argue with God, to go to Him and say "Lord, why have you done this, why have you allowed this to happen?" Part of that maturity is being able to say "I've brought it before you, I've heard your answer, and now I accept it. Give me the grace to obey you". God is not against us going to Him and yet so often we are afraid of being honest with Him. I've learnt the best way to accept what God is doing is first of all to ask him if it really is His

[23] Job 38:1-42:6

will. Learning this was a hard lesson. After that tremendous night, the shoulder didn't get any better. It would have been nice to write that from that day on I didn't have any trouble. We like happy endings, they encourage us and make us feel good inside. In the long run there is a happy ending for all those who believe in Jesus Christ, but in between are all the obstacles that can trip us up; the things that should go right but somehow don't, the problems that ought to go away but seem to hang on. The truth is that the shoulder didn't improve, no matter how much we prayed, and I have to say a lot of prayer was put in by all concerned.

The breakthrough came on a quiet day, a quiet enforced by college, difficult, since being quiet has never been my strong point! These came up once a term when we were encouraged to pray, reflect, read and also receive some spiritual teaching from a guest speaker. To be honest, I found them hard to get into, but once you got used to them they were really good, for it gave me time to be alone with God. I found it quite useful to read a short epistle and then allow God to speak to me through it. That done, it became an open agenda for God to speak to me, or for me to seek God about certain situations in my life at that time.

It's very important when we spend time with God that we don't go in with a fixed agenda, but actually allow time for Him to raise issues. This can be frightening, because God may say things we don't really want to hear, but when that happens it's because we need to hear it. Our quiet day that particular term was the beginning of March. As it was not too bad outside, I asked someone to take me into the grounds and come back later, hoping they wouldn't forget, or it might turn into a quiet day with fasting!

Now there were two things on my agenda. The first was

the future, as in the second year you are supposed to begin thinking about the next step. Usually this means a curacy, but for me this was different. I'd already begun the long process of writing to various organisations to ask if there was a place for someone like me. The second item was my shoulder. I felt it was really time to ask the Lord what was going on. Was he going to heal it? Why hadn't he? What was I going to make of it? Now I'm not one to beat around the bush, so the first question was "Lord, are you going to heal my shoulder?" "Yes" he replied. So far, so good, I thought, "eventually". What did he mean by "eventually?" Why not now? How much longer had I to wait? What about the pain? "It's a nuisance, why won't you take it away?" I could feel my temperature rising. I didn't understand. "Surely you take away problems, why 'eventually'?" God said "Do you trust me, Alyn?" Well, yes of course, I did. "If I allow your shoulder to continue hurting, will you still love me?" I didn't feel I could answer at that moment. He went on to tell me my shoulder would not interfere with my preaching. This was important as there was a mission coming up and I was on the team. He then led me to a passage of scripture[24] where Paul talks about his afflictions, how he too had a problem, how he had prayed "three times", and yet the Lord had not taken the problem away. I could certainly indentify with that. Then He led me to words that I'd never read before but which have become important ever since. They ran "My grace is sufficient for you. My strength is made perfect in your weakness".

For the time being He left it at that. I had an important question to think about. Could I love God in this situation? Could I trust Him? Apparently He was calling me to go through this pain, yet at the same time I couldn't forget what He'd already done, and what He'd promised to do. Could I love God? – Yes! He hadn't changed. What

[24] 2 Cor.12:7-10

needed to change was my attitude. Hadn't I got to the stage where everything had become easy? Pray to God, and he'd take it away. "Lord, I've got a headache. Take it away". "Lord, I need this, Lord, I need that". Yet the reality is very different. People we prayed for didn't necessarily get better, some died. If I could trust God to give me the things that were good, then I also had to trust Him in the things that were not so good. And so I said "Yes, I do still love you" and I hope, pray and believe that that day I took a step to maturity.

– THIRTEEN –

I have to say the shoulder didn't improve but God kept His promise. Time and time again when the shoulder was really painful, a prayer calmed it down. I noticed that whenever I was about to do something for the Lord, the pain increased. I didn't believe in coincidences. The enemy has many ways of tripping us up, but in Jesus Christ they come to nothing. We had a terrific mission where I made lots of friends. It was a wonderful time of seeing the Lord work, not only changing lives, but in bringing a unity to the churches, because at one stage it looked as if the whole thing would collapse, and there wouldn't be a mission at all. Of course the enemy did play one or two tricks. I developed a whitlow on my finger, which had to be lanced, very painfully. Not easy when you then have to give a talk straight afterwards. My hosts very kindly washed my clothes and hung them out to dry, only to discover that one pair of jeans had been pinched. However, I was more than compensated for this by seeing people give their lives to Jesus, either for the first time, or a fresh start.

And so, back to college. Exams, a placement in a hospital, studying, clinics and at the end of the summer term, a month in my parish placement. During this time I learnt to be at ease with pain. I learnt to trust God whenever it was bad. I learnt to trust Him in other things, as well, like the time when the amplifier broke down, when I was due to preach. That morning I had a really bad sore throat, yet people heard. And there was another thing I had to trust God for. That was my Dad, because his health was becoming a serious concern. Whatever else I thought about him, he was still my Dad. Our relationship hadn't been particularly good, in fact it was really at its best when there were quite a few miles between us. Dad was the kind of person who put everybody else first. Unfortunately, sometimes it felt as if the family came nowhere on his list of priorities, though I've discovered that wasn't true at all. The problem was one of communication.

Sometimes the people that we love most are the people we find it hardest to express that love to. I'm pretty sure that Dad loved all of us, but just had a strange way of expressing it. At the same time, I've learnt to appreciate the fact that he didn't spoil us. We didn't get everything we wanted, when we wanted it, and sometimes we didn't get anything at all. When you're in that situation you don't appreciate it. It's only afterwards that you see the benefits. There were special moments, like going to Buckingham Palace. (I'm pretty sure he was more excited than I was), even more so was the day we returned to York for my graduation. There are so many things about that day that I'll never forget, especially going to York Minster in the evening and hearing David Watson speak. I believe that Dad believed in God. He was always willing to go to church on Christmas Eve with me, but really I'm talking about the last days of our relationship. Before that I had so much resentment, anger and bitterness against him. I didn't want to be compared with him or even talk about him, but praise God, Jesus came and took away all that antagonism in 1978.

I'm not pretending after that things were superb, there were still tensions, but by the grace of God, I learnt to understand him, and we could talk and argue without tempers flaring. In fact, I had a suspicion I actually got to like being with him, and was hoping this was going to develop into something really good, and that he would be around for a few years, but I was wrong.

– FOURTEEN –

The first signs of the crisis came in the summer of 1979. Dad was taken into hospital. Although from time to time Dad moaned about being ill, it was actually a rare occurrence for him to stop his activities. He had been having pains that were getting steadily worse. He wasn't in for long, but by the time he came out I could see the change. Some of the energy and spark had gone and he had some discomfort. Later he discovered that an operation would be dicey as his heart was weak, and despite his assurances to the contrary I felt he was deteriorating.

I remember Christmas 1979 particularly. He had to have a long rest and just sat quietly. He kept working, but never seemed to be quite the same, and hospitalization occurred several times during that year. During August 1980 I was in Wales doing outreach and teaching. It is really strange, but one particular weekend I was unsettled, and indeed physically discomfitted. There were many reasons for that. My health wasn't brilliant, and our accommodation wasn't all that you might expect. It was also a damp summer! Nevertheless, I still believe there was some connection between that weekend and the phone call on the Monday to say Dad had had a severe heart attack. As he was not expected to live, I was to ring the hospital straight away.

I spoke to Tony my brother who explained the situation to me. It was difficult. Here I was, stuck in the middle of Wales, wondering if I should go home, whether I would ever see Dad again, and worst of all, how would I cope if he died. Tony suggested that rushing back wasn't a good idea. If it was to happen, it would happen, and we would take it from there. One of the special things was that I was among christian brothers and sisters who immediately sought God, who said stay and trust. That night I had to speak to a young peoples' group. I felt heavy, tired, downcast, and yet while it wasn't the most lively meeting I have been involved in, the Lord gave me the ability to speak, encourage and challenge. I know that other people's prayers played a very important part. That's why it's so important to pray for each other, for in prayer we really enter into each others situations and wrestle together.

I had some wrestling to do on the Tuesday. There were some real crunch questions to bring before God. There had been no news overnight or during the morning, but after lunch there was a glimmer of hope. Dad was hanging on. Praise the Lord for that, but I still had to seek the Lord as to whether this was the right place for me to be. Spending time with the Lord, in prayer, can be good. It can also be life changing. On this particular occasion I emerged in a totally different frame of mind than that which I'd entered in. The Lord had definitely told me to stay where I was, and continue the work of Jesus.

It is great to know we can really meet with God and He can deal with our hurts and turn us round. So many things happened in the space of twenty minutes. First of all there were the doubts. If you're feeling shaky, just know that at the name of Jesus, every knee shall bow. I know where the doubts were coming from. Remember Job "He'll curse you if you let anything happen to him[25]". We have authority in the name of Jesus to dismiss the enemy, the accuser, and I did just that. Already I was feeling better. Once we know this, we're able to realize that God only wants the best for us. That doesn't mean every situation we get into is going to work out the way we hope it will, but we do have a God we can trust, and know that He will work it out for good. All we need to do is to speak honestly to Him. I said "God, you can heal or maybe you won't. I'm asking you in the name of Jesus for a miracle".

[25] Job 1:11 (Author's paraphrase)

– FIFTEEN –

When you've really opened your heart to God, and asked Him for what you want, there is nothing else that you can do other than trust Him and wait and see what happens. In the next few weeks the news was good. By the end of the first week Dad was off the danger list, and in a way no news became good news. He seemed to be making steady progress. There were other benefits from that meeting with God. I was recharged, rekindled, and had a new power within me. Even my own physical problems cleared up. It taught me to be responsible in letting someone know where I was at any time. Prior to this, I would just take off, and if I remembered, send a postcard.

By the time I arrived home after the Greenbelt Festival, Dad was making slow but steady progress. That night, my miracle was fulfilled, and I was able to go and see him. We had a good time together, and when I visited on the Friday the news was even better. He would be out at the weekend, or possibly early the next week. For the time being, the crisis was over and the Lord's command to stay in Wales was proved to be right.

The next few weeks were taken up preparing for my final year at college and spending two days a week on placement. The placement was in a very deprived area of Nottingham with many problems, expecially unemployment and lack of social amenities. It brought me face to face with other kinds of suffering, of lives broken by povery and powerlessness and a sense of worthlessness. I was also confronted by situations that didn't change, in a sense a bit like mine, yet often without the hope of Jesus. Yet they were good people, people who were open to Jesus. I remember many special occasions such as the day we went on a coach trip to Belton House, and the services arranged for the local infant schoool which I had responsibility for organising. I remember that particularly because the service was held the day after Dad died. A few days before I had spoken to Dad on the telephone and he told me he was having to go back into hospital. He told me not to worry, it was just to make some adjustments to his drug regime. I told him that I loved him, and that I'd be thinking about him and praying for him.

That was the last time we spoke, but when I arrived home after the first day of term my brother was waiting for me. I think I already knew why, and as I think back I am sure God had been preparing me, yet it still came as a shock. Tony spent a little time with me and then went home. I'd often wondered how I'd react. It wasn't a new experience, after all, through the years I'd lost quite a few close friends, but there is a difference when it's someone in your family. When you've been used to the idea of them always being there. It's difficult to come to terms with the fact that you'll never see them again this side of eternity. It's hard to describe how I felt – not angry, not questioning, half realising that it was probably the best thing that could have happened. Just numb, aware that things were going on around me and yet not wanting to do anything, just sitting there in darkness, thinking, praying, and nervously resting in God, looking to Him for what I needed. At the same time I was hurting because if I felt like that, then for Mum, Tony my brother, Frankie, my sister and their children could be much worse. Could they find the comfort I had?

– SIXTEEN –

Altogether I must have sat there for 3 hours. Praise God for part of the time I had Margaret with me, a friend I could talk to, and someone to help me tell people who needed to know, like my tutor at college, and close friends.

When Margaret had gone I just sat alone. The worst part is telling people, because each time its like re-opening a wound, reliving the pain. However, I have a wonderful family in God who I know were supporting me in prayer, but what about the children's service the next day? Could I go through with it? Yes, in the power of Jesus, I could or would. I would keep going because that was the best thing to do. It wasn't easy, but then you wouldn't expect it to be. The service was a success. I managed to fulfil all that was asked of me that day. Of the days that followed, leading up to the funeral, I have to praise God for his mercy, grace and strength, expecially on the day of the funeral.

While I want to remember always the things that Dad did, for a number of reasons, that day I want to forget. It's an old cliche that time heals, but it's true, at least in part. It should be "time and Jesus heal". I thank God for the fact that many of my friends at college offered me transport to go to see Mum, and also for their love as I slowly began to get back into college life. After all, my first day at college that year had been a good one, and I believed there were going to be many good days to follow. Apart from college work a lot of my time that term was spent in writing letters. I had a painful awareness that in less than year I'd have left college. The way already seemed uncertain. If I was looking for some comfort, I was not going to get any.

It is no exaggeration to say that over the last few years I have written hundreds of letters, looking for the right place. Now I discovered that if getting into college had been a major problem, then finding the place to exercise the ministry God had given me was one of much larger proportions, and not so easily solved. The letters weren't unsympathetic but it was either a case of lack of resources, lack of suitable accommodation or lack of vision. If you have the idea that people with disabilities are not able to contribute, it's hard to be suddenly confronted by the opposite idea. Furthermore, if your view of ministry is such that only able-bodied people can serve God then you are not open to other possibilities and that openness is the key. Nobody, including myself, was suggesting that I become ordained and become a priest or curate, but the bible makes it quite clear that these aren't the only ministries within the church. You only need to look at Paul's letters to the Romans, Corinthians and Ephesians[26] to see how diverse ministry can be. Trying to encourage this diversity is a major task. I remember Roy Catchpole, the vicar of the parish where I was training, saying in a television programme that there were things I wouldn't be able to do, and he was right, except that his picture of the role of a minister was based on the premise that the vicar has to be able to do everything.

Paul gives us a different picture. He says some are cal-

[26] Rom.12 1 Cor.12-14 Eph.4

led to be apostles, some evangelists, some teachers etc, and praise God the church is waking up to the fact that the minister shouldn't be expected to be good at everything, and do everything. However, given the biblical picture there were still problems. If I were to exercise ministry it might not fit into the biblical framework. In fact it might not fit into any existing pattern at all. That might mean braking new gound and using innovations. That is a very threatening situation to most churches. There was a dilemma. How was I to approach different organisations? Either I could start off by saying that I believed God had given me these gifts or this ministry, and then mentioning, as subtely as possible, that I was disabled, or lived in a wheelchair most of the time. Or I could say that I was in a wheelchair but I could do this or that – were they interested? I think it is a Catch 22 situation! Either they switched off right at the beginning, or at the point where I mentioned wheelchairs. By Christmas things didn't look too good at all. I was even getting to the stage where I could almost guess what the letter would say: "We're interested but . . . however we do wish you ever success". Christmas 1980 looked as if it would be quite bleak and 1981 didn't look as if it would be much better, except that it was the International Year of Disabled People. Maybe that would help, maybe it wouldn't. I'd just have to trust God, and wait and see.

– SEVENTEEN –

Trusting God needs to become a habit – and it works! Towards the end of term things started to pick up. I got an enquiry from the BBC about the possibility of doing a television programme about Easter. I also had a letter from the diocese of Coventry. A parish was interested in seeing if there was a place for me. The programme was to link in with the International Year of Disabled People and over the next couple of months I had conversations with researchers, and tape tests to see if my voice would come across. I remember the tape test particularly, because I had just come back from a mission in York. This had been good in many ways, but once again the problems of disability were highlighted. The difficulties were not of access, or facilities, but simply of communication. It was a great thrill to be based in my old college, yet I was a little surprised that apart from staff who knew me, I'd really got to build relationships again.

I was confronted by the same old prejudices, assumptions and misconceptions, that I'd encountered first as a student seven years before. It was made clear to me that the only way to break down barriers was by constant contact between disabled and able-bodied people. The difference this time was that whereas seven years earlier I'd had plenty of time to get to know people, this time I had only a week to break down barriers, and to share the good news of Jesus, and I'll tell you what, God did some amazing things that week. I met and spoke to a lot of people, which on the face of it, at the beginning of the week, had looked almost impossible.

Unfortunately, the possibility of going to Coventry didn't work out, but other doors were opening. The television programme would be a way of not only witnessing about Jesus, but of raising issues about how a person like myself could exercise his call to ministry. Naturally here were problems. Having kept us waiting while they decided whether to film the programme or not, we were given only 24 hours notice before filming was to begin. As usual, I was ill! There followed two days of hectic activity which included working in the parish, reading a lesson in the weekly communion service at college, a long interview, and an attempt at singing in front of the camera!

None of these is easy when you've got a sore throat and a cold, especially when the parish work involved going door-to-door on snow-covered streets, with a camera crew trailing you. The lesson was read against a background of tension due to the fact that the BBC were not too popular in college at that time. Still, we got through it, and I had to admit the worst point was when they said "can you sing us a song?". The first recording didn't go two well, because we forgot to take my glasses off. My right hand had a habit of coming and removing the glasses rather violently. I guess you could say it's making a right spectacle of yourself! However, the second time went well, although in no way could I vouch for those listening! At the end of filming we could only wait and pray that the film would come out to the glory of God.

Life went on, with finals approaching, deadlines to meet

for pieces of work, and Easter. Although getting a job was proving to be a problem, at least for the time being invitations to speak were coming in. I felt quite strongly that this was probably an indication for the future. Nevertheless there had to be a breakthrough. If I were to be ordained, and exercise a ministry, I had to be able to point to experience, to say "look – it does work" and to do that I needed to be placed where that could happen, so it all hinged on the next stage. Where was God going to put me, and what was I going to do?

– EIGHTEEN –

A possible answer came suddenly. A church in Liverpool was interested in my being a voluntary lay worker, and one Friday in April, John, my helper and I set off for the North.

On the way there I came face to face with the realization that if this was the next step it would mean a completely new way of life. It would mean leaving the security of the hostel, the fellowship of my church, and going to a completely new set of people. The Lord reminded me of Abraham and how he was first called to go [27]. He didn't know where he was going or how, except that the Lord would bless him and all those who came into contact with him. The difference was that I had hindsight. I knew that God had kept his promise to Abraham, and that He could do it for me. It wasn't really an interview as such but rather informal discussions, and the end result looked quite promising. It would be a good situation to go into, with a fair amount of freedom to develop my own areas of ministry and interests. I would be a community service volunteer, but attached to the parish, being looked after by other community service volunteers.

On the way home I certainly felt encouraged and

[27] Gen.12:1-5

excited, but there were a number of things that needed to happen. We would just have to wait and see what the Lord had in mind. For the time being there were more immediate things to consider, such as exams, and making travel plans as I was now getting even more invitations to go and speak, especially at conferences. It was also coming towards the end of my placement. A time for farewells and reflection, and I remember thinking on my last day that on the one hand, yes, some of the people I had met had moved on in some ways and yet in many other ways they were still in the same physical conditions, still faced with the same struggle to live, and perhaps in some cases their material situations had deteriorated. Their sufferings were not necessarily spiritual, although in some ways they were, but they seemed to be trapped in a system that kept them down, depriving them of power and provision. Into this the message of Jesus had to come, because God does care, but at that stage I found it difficult to convey how, so I left with mixed feelings. I'd learnt a lot, I'd enjoyed being there, but I was also painfully aware that for many the suffering would continue. Only knowing Jesus can make a difference as to how we cope with ongoing pain.

– NINETEEN –

It's all very well to proclaim victory even if we know it's true, but one of the biggest problems to Christians is to relate the victory of Jesus on the Cross to the trials and tribulations that we face every day. It's an even bigger problem to those who don't know Jesus. Certainly the question I get asked more than anything is "If God loves you, why?" "Why does he allow you to go through pain? Why has He allowed that problem to happen? Why doesn't the Church accept you? Why are you still in wheelchair? Surely God heals?"

Have you ever noticed when you think life should be easy, things start falling apart. When everything seems to be under control, suddenly there's a new problem. When I was a child I suffered from asthma, in fact all of our family seem to be weak when it comes to respiratory matters. I remember some really bad attacks when I was in my early teens, times when I just couldn't catch my breath, made worse by the panic. When I became a Christian this disappeared. I had very few problems, apart from pneumonia at the age of 16 in 1968, until the summer of 1981. Then all sorts of things happened.

At first I thought it was just a cold, and that it would

pass. I was sneezing and wheezing, and feeling uncomfortable day after day, and as June went on it seemed to get worse. There were two problems – in the day time some kind of irritation that affected my sinuses and caused so much sneezing, and at night when the air went cold I was short of breath. Needless to say, I tried all kinds of treatments to bring it under control without much success. It was beginning to get a real pain, especially when I was speaking or preaching because it just felt as if my nostrils were full of cotton wool. Eventually I went to see the doctor and discovered it was in fact hay fever and related allergies. It was prayed for, but it's still there, and once again it seemed as if the Lord was saying "you can cope with it" and in fact it's true.

On many occasions when I've been feeling really bad, and about to speak, I've apologized afterwards only to be told that my speech was perfectly clear. But why did it come back, and why does God allow me to go through all this? I believe it's because Jesus made it quite clear that we would have problems[28]. Real Christian living means coming to terms with the situation we are in. You see, there is only one reality, that Jesus on the cross defeated all sin, death and disease. He broke their power and handed the victory to the disciples, and through them, to us[29]. Nowhere in the Gospels does Jesus imply that we will not have problems. Indeed, he says exactly the opposite. To be honest we would all like our Christian lives to be easy. I can remember a friend of mine pulling me up for something I said. I was saying that Jesus offers a free gift with no strings attached. My friend said "that's not true!" Not totally. Now it is true that salvation is a gift because we can't earn it, we can't buy it and we can't save ourselves. Only Jesus and what he did on the cross can do that. However, when we accept that gift, usually we make a commitment to follow Him, and Jesus himself made it

 [28] Jn.16:33 [29] 1 Cor.15:57

quite clear what that means: "If any man would follow me, then he must take up his cross daily"[30]. This is a personal cross, because for all of us there are parts of our lives that we would rather forget about.

There are situations we'd rather not be in. When Jesus prayed "if there is any other way let this cup pass by"[31] he meant it. He knew full well that if he did drink from that cup it would mean pain, death, desertion, rejection and that moment when for the first time in his life, because of our sin, He would be cut off from God. Yet he drank from the cup. He took it on knowing this was planned from eternity. The cross was no accident or miscalculation. When we decide to follow Jesus, we take on whatever lies ahead. Praise God that for most of us we don't have to go all the way to the cross as Jesus did, but some might and some do, so let's not pretend or be surprised when things do happen[32].

I have no idea why I developed asthma or hay fever at that point in my life. I have a few indications. I know that the enemy is quite happy to use it[33] both physically to try and disrupt me and emotionally and spiritual to try and drag me down and sow the seeds of doubt. However, I know that God's power is greatest in my weakness[34]. I have to learn to trust Him, because it's at that point that the victory we proclaim and the sufferings we experience come together[35]. Either He will take away my problem or He will give me enough grace and strength to cope and overcome it. The result is the same. The enemy is defeated and Jesus has won.

[30] Mk.8:34 (Author's precis) [31] Lk.22:42-44 (Author's precis)
[32] 1 Pe.4:12 [33] 1 Pe.5:8 [34] 2 Cor.12:10 [35] 1 Pe.4:19

PART III

WAITING IN THE WINGS

I am waiting in the wings
For my time to arrive
I am feeling dead inside
But you make me alive
Disappointment and frustration
Are hard to bear
But I know I will cope
If you are there
So I am waiting in the wings
For that special day
When you will clear the obstacles
Out of my way

– TWENTY –

Having left college, I anticipated moving to Liverpool in the near future, and looking forward to a new life, confident that this was the next stage in my journey, but I was wrong! It looked as if 1982 was going to be an exciting year. Due to my surprising success (surprise on my part!) in the England team (for athletics and football) the year before, I'd been picked to go to Denmark. My health was fairly good and there were just enough engagements to keep me going until my anticipated move. Then problems started to arise.

A lengthy local government strike in Liverpool halted my accommodation and everything ground to a halt. Still, I was pretty sure that once the strike ended we'd soon be back on the way. At the beginning of Holy Week I went to speak in Rugby. The weather was fine, I felt good, the meeting had gone well, and I returned hope optimistic. One of the things about tragedies is that they are usually sudden and unexpected. When I arrived home there was the usual stack of mail, amongst which was a letter from the County Council. I thought it might be encouraging news. In fact it was the opposite. Due to the financial situation the County Council felt unable to support me in

Liverpool. This had been one of the key factors to my going there.

I telephoned Liverpool that night. They weren't too pleased, and for the first time my optimism began to dwindle. Two days later the new Rector of West Bridgford came to see me about my lay readership training. In York I'd been asked to take up training and had been accepted by the Bishop of Selby, but had left before completion. My church were very happy to recommend me for further training. I'd had an interview with one of our Bishops while at St. John's, who again said that I was ideal for training. However, from that point on nothing happened. Despite repeated enquiries we could get no information. Now with the appointment of a new rector I started all over again to try and get a decision.

All in all it was quite a friendly encounter, but it was felt that lay readership was not an appropriate ministry for me. No specific reasons were given, but I had an idea that it was mainly due to my disability. He told me that I would be allowed to preach at my own church occasionally. To say I was disappointed would be an understatement. I've never been able to work out how God can call you through one Bishop and turn you down through another, without specific reasons I couldn't even mount an appeal.

I was becoming painfully aware that my disability was going to be a real problem, as far as my ministry was concerned. It seemed that within this diocese there was no opening at all, and I must be content with a few odd crumbs now and then, but worse was to come. On Good Friday I received a letter from the vicar of the church in Liverpool. It was a kind letter in many ways, but what it mounted to was that due to many circumstances I could not go there. It had turned out to be quite a week. How was I to make sense of it, and what was God saying about my ministry?

– TWENTY-ONE –

It's hard to put into words how I felt, but I'll have a go. The first feeling was of utter rejection. It seemed that despite the fact that God had called me, no-one wanted to know. The Diocese didn't, Liverpool didn't, and as far as I could tell, nobody else did.

I started to question whether God had really called me, whether I had made some mistake, and I asked Him to explain it to me. I sat in silence reading, praying, thinking. Being Good Friday, the lessons were all concerned with Cavalry, with Jesus' rejection, isolation and pain. Did he feel like I did? Did he wonder what it had all been for? What about the disciples, how did they feel watching the man they admired, loved and had given up everything for, dying in agony on a pice of wood? What of their hopes and dreams? What of my hopes, now crushed? In the space of five days everything that concerned my future had just gone.

At that point there didn't seem to be anything to replace it, because even while waiting to go to Liverpool I'd been writing to other organisations without success. College were very good in supporting me. They appealed through newsletters and other connections, but there was just nothing. In the afternoon I went to church to help with the children's service. It lifted me a little, but I still felt broken and bruised. I was at least able to ask some friends to pray.

However, there was one difference between myself and the disciples. As on the first day when I went to Liverpool, again I had hindsight. You see, despite the fact that Jesus had said so, the disciples didn't know what was to happen next [36]. All they could see was the gloom, despair and sorrow, as they saw the one they had loved buried in a tomb. They didn't know that two days later Jesus would come back to life. Mary didn't know when she went to the tomb on the Sunday morning that the stone would be moved away and the tomb empty![37] She wasn't looking for a risen Jesus when she saw the gardener. She was looking for someone she had loved dearly, who was no longer alive. Mary wasn't expecting to hear a familiar voice when she asked the gardener where the body was, but then she heard it – "Mary" – and she knew that Jesus had risen. Later that day two disciples on a journey discovered Him in the breaking of bread[38]. In the evening a bunch of frightened people were hiding behind closed doors, panicking at every sound, and thinking of the rumours about an empty tomb and missing body. Suddenly He was there, saying "Peace"[39]. They didn't know that that would happen, but I knew it had and I knew that no matter how bad Friday had been, Sunday was coming.

 [36] Jn.19 [37] Jn.20:1-11 [38] Lk.24:13-35 [39] Jn.20:19-23

– TWENTY-TWO –

It would be nice to be able to say that suddenly everything changed, but it wasn't quite like that, at least nothing tangible. Nevertheless, by Sunday I felt very different. That was confirmed later on in the week when I received a letter from a parish in Cambridge. They asked if I'd like to go down and explore the possibility of some kind of ministry. I was excited about this, but I'd learnt my lesson – it might come to nothing. It was just a sign, a reminder that God was in control and fitted in with the way I felt. I'm pretty sure that the disciples didn't understand the full implication of Jesus' resurrection. They just knew He was alive and rejoiced at that. In the same way, although I knew several doors had closed, another door had opened. I could rejoice at that. I no longer felt isolated and alone. Like the disciples, my hope was reborn.

What followed was a period of waiting. What was beyond dispute was that apart from Cambridge, nothing was opening up at present. It was this period that lasted for nearly two years. Occasionally there would be hopeful signs, but nothing concrete. There were days of waiting, hoping the phone would ring, or that there would be a letter. Long days, days which in one sense felt as though they were wasted, and only the knowledge of God's love contradicted that. There were the times when I went out to various events, met people, reminded them that I was available for speaking opportunities, times when I received vague encouragement which usually came to nothing.

It's hard when you wake up, feeling that this is the day, that something positive is going to happen, and go to bed thinking that maybe it will be tomorrow. I don't want you to get the idea that I was simply sitting around passively; I was always on the lookout for possibilities, vacancies. I wrote many letters, but while the responses were kind, they all came down to the same thing "Sorry but we don't feel there is a place for you here". Of course, there were high spots. The trip to Cambridge seemed to go quite well, despite hay fever. The World Championships in Denmark brought some success with two bronze medals.

Many friends shared my frustrations. Tony Evans, who is now with the Lord, spent many hours talking with me, encouraging me, and trying to open doors. I am so grateful for his friendship and ministry. Phil, my friend from York, and Don and Freda, who live quite close by and whom I've known for many years, all shared with me during this time of frustration and waiting, hoping that eventually doors would open. However, by July nothing seemed to be happening. Yes, indeed, I had to just hold on, and trust.

– TWENTY-THREE –

With the summer came new opportunities and problems. I was asked by Phil to be assistant chaplain on a youth camp. I have to say it wasn't one of the best weeks of weather in that year! This was one event in a busy summer, culminating at Green belt, where for the first time I was actually going to perform – not on the main stage, of course, but on the fringe. I asked Pete, a friend, to sing some songs I'd written, while I would do my best to recite some poetry. However, the enemy decided to have a go, and during my last few days at the Ranch I became ill. The diagnosis was viral tonsillitis. Perhaps he wanted to keep me quiet! My last two days there were not at all good. I felt weak, washed out and not really in any condition to go camping for four days. I was so ill I was in no condition to leave on Thursday, the appointed day. In fact on the Friday other people were going down, which was better, as they could at least look after me on the train.

The performance was to be on the Monday afternoon, but I honestly had grave doubts as to whether I'd be fit enough to do anything. The real problem wasn't physical, but emotional. I'd just felt this was the last straw. Why had God allowed this? I'd done so much that summer, witnessing God's love and care, why now? What was it all about? Yet the enemy didn't have a victory. On the Wednesday evening I passed out at the tea table, but the Lord gave me renewed strength to take a meeting in the evening. On the Thursday, despite the fact that I wasn't supposed to be there, I was asked to do the epilogue after the barbecue. People said it was very clear. Praise God, because it was in the open air, not easy for me at any time.

On the Saturday, Phil and I went to a wedding, where I discovered temporary relief – a couple of glasses of wine certainly made me feel much better. (Perhaps Paul was right when he suggested this to Timothy!). On the Monday, the rain held off long enough for us to give our performance. Towards the end of that weekend I came to an understanding that it didn't matter what the problems were, God was greater. Whatever I faced I just had to trust God and know that it would work out. I needed to know that because after a busy summer I was going back to more frustration.

There wasn't going to be any immediate change. The only notable thing about the Autumn of 1982 was that I finally finished the first draft of "Freedom Ride". Yet in saying that, I am aware of just how miraculously that had been done. As I hadn't had regular writing slots, the book had had to be fitted in amongst other things, ten minutes here, half an hour there, sometimes a whole hour, yet despite my initial misgivings, every time I started, the Holy Spirit gave me words. Now began the task of rewriting and editing, and in between, always the waiting and hoping. Maybe tomorrow . . .

– TWENTY-FOUR –

I enjoy going to weddings, especially when it's a close friend and this time even more so because I'd played a very small part in how it came about. It really went back to Greenbelt. Pete, who had sung the songs, bumped into an old friend, and the result was the wedding. My part was that if I hadn't asked him to sing, he probably wouldn't have been there. It was quite a weekend. I'd been out on the Friday evening, and then had to get up early on the Saturday, to go into London to get out to Buckinghamshire. I'd arranged to meet another friend at St. Pancras.

It was a really good day, but on the way back I noticed that my wrist was aching. The following day it seemed to be much worse, in fact, I couldn't use my hand at all. By the end of the day I had it strapped up, hoping that this would solve the problem. It didn't, and over the next few days it became even more painful. I could not work out what I had done. I didn't remember banging it, catching it, or anything like that. Now no injury comes at a good time, but this brought my progress to a halt. You see, it was the one part of my life that was looking really good. I was beginning to do things that I'd never been able to do before – for example, take off my bed cover, open my bed, take off most of my clothes once the buttons or zips had been dealt with, clean my teeth, open doors and many other small things.

They were tangible signs of God's healing, steps that meant progress, and indications that very soon I might be able to live independently. One of the desires of my heart was to have a place of my own – a home, where I could be myself, where I could live my own life more fully. Ever since I'd come to the hostel I'd had one aim – to leave! This was not because I didn't like the place, I did, not because I felt restricted, as on the whole I had a fair amount of freedom.

When I first went to the hostel it was a new concept – a place where young independent-minded people with disabilities could have control over their lives, make their own decisions, and within reason develop their own daily routine. However, I'd always regarded it as a step on the way, because I believed "with God, all things are possible", and that there are no limitations other than the ones He gives. I'd already begun to make enquiries about moving out, looking at the possibilities, what kind of accommodation, what help would I need, and most importantly, what could I do for myself? I believed that the more I could do, the better my opportunities would be. Now, suddenly, even this dream seemed to be going wrong.

– TWENTY-FIVE –

I really wondered what was going on. I believe it's healthy to actually confront God because there are times when it seems to be one problem after another. Blind obedience and deep trust are all right up to a point, but for a Christian in relationship with God it's legitimate to say "isn't this enough?" You go through the options: sin, disobedience, or just plain fellowship. When the answer to these is "NO" you begin to wonder what else it can be. Within a very short space of time I couldn't do anything.

It was so frustrating, and what's more, there was pain. Mind you, I didn't just sit back – I attempted to carry on, keep life ticking over. Sometimes there were very costly victories. A task that normally took two minutes took over half an hour and more often than not I had to admit defeat. Once again the pain caused its own vicious circle, culminating in tension and increased spasm. In many ways the next few months were a low spot. invitations to speak were few and far between; "Freedom Ride" was in the process of being rewritten and edited, but it became clear it wasn't going to be easy to get it published. Already, from the samples I'd sent out, I was receiving discouraging though not unkind comments.

My health was poor, and time just seemed to drag, so much so that I turned back to studying, returning to the OU in order to complete my degree. It wasn't all bad though. There was an exciting return trip to Bristol despite pains in my wrist and over the early spring there were signs of new life. There was an invitation to take part in a holiday mission during the summer at Dawlish Warren in Devon, the completion and typing of "Freedom Ride", and the possibility of a trip to America the following year. My athletic performances continued to go well! Plans for a support group were taking shape. A group of friends would promote the ministry God had given me, and with God's guidance seek to open more doors.

Along with the signs of hope were the ongoing frustrations. I continued to apply for jobs without success; there was a possibility of going to Grimsby to be part of a team ministry, but it came to nothing as did the previous opening in Cambridge. Publishers didn't like my book. Either they didn't think it would sell, or they believed it would need extensive rewriting before being acceptable. Worst of all, there were two missions due to take place during the summer. I had applied to help on both, without success. I attended the meetings of the first one in West Bridgford. As for the second one, I did not even receive a reply, although I knew they were in need of people. I suppose in the end I just gave it to the Lord. Surely things would soon change.

PART IV

LIVING IN THE GAP

I've heard your word
And done my best
I've toiled hard
And now I rest
Changes will come
Ups and downs
But you will keep my feet
On solid ground
So I'm living in the gap
Far from home
Holding onto your promise
Until I see it come

– TWENTY-SIX –

The summer of 1983 was the beginning of a new era. First of all, there was a new book of poetry. I was quite excited, because we'd found a new publisher that would give us a much wider distribution. I see poetry as part of the ministry God has given me, and so to be able to share that ministry with many more people seemed right. After this we received notification from the BBC that they were going to repeat my programme about Easter. This was good, it would be another chance to witness some new responses. There were the summer activities, including a new experience – two weeks on the Devon coast at Dawlish Warren, and of course Greenbelt, where once again Phil and I were going to inflict poetry and music on anyone who stood around the fringe! Dawlish Warren is a seaside resort just outside Exeter where for two weeks the Holiday Mission organises outreach.

My invitation had come partly as a result of the youth camp a year earlier, and from Phil and friends. Phil had told me what a wonderful time he'd had the previous year. I had met many of the team, having been invited to their reunion and to preach in the Autumn. It didn't really hit me what the accommodation would be like until I actually arrived and realised with horror that I'd be spending two weeks sleeping in a tent! Remember the youth camp a year before! However, God was gracious and we coped. The same was true for Greenbelt which was five nights at the most, but two weeks! When you can't use a camp bed, and when you discover the first night you can't even stay on a li-lo! The discovery of this was quite daunting. The problem is that when I sleep I like to have something solid at the back of me so that if I roll, there is a limit to how far I go.

In a tent you don't have that, expecially in a big tent. Praise God it was a dry night, because I rolled off the li-lo and out of the tent! "Oh, great" I thought. I was already having great problems sleeping due to the proximity of the mainline to Exeter and the fairly frequent 125's whistling past my ears! Now I was looking up at the stars! Still, I'd been assured that all I had to do was call and someone would come to my aid.

After a few minutes I decided it was maybe time to get some sleep, preferably inside. There were three others in the tent, a call was bound to wake at least one of them, so I called, and waited, then shouted again, and waited! After about a quarter of an hour of this I began to realise that no-one on the site, let alone in the tent, was going to wake up. After about twenty minutes this was confirmed. Now the horror really sank in. Two weeks of this! With a great deal of effort I managed to shuffle back into the tent. Not easy when you're tightly zipped into a sleeping bag. Unfortunately though there was no way I could get back on the li-lo.

My fears grew even worse the following night when we were rained out and had to sleep in the hall. Still, at least now there were only twelve nights to go. But you know it's when we are at our weakest that God has a habit of coming good. I'm not saying that after that it was plain sailing.

Far from it. I had asthma, hay-fever attacks, and you can be sure that conditions on the whole weren't that suited to a wheelchair, but by the end of the two weeks, there was no doubt that I would be back next year, God willing. Undoubtedly the most exciting thing was how God had spoken through my weakness and disability. I was beginning to learn.

Those of you wondering about my wrist need to know that there was no rapid improvement, but I was learning that even in this, God was in control. During the few months before going to Dawlish there had been one or two problems. Early in the spring I had one of my best ever days in athletics. I didn't realise at the time that it would be the last time I would compete without some kind of problem. By the time the National championships came round I had a serious dilemma. A week before, I'd had an accident. I fell off the toilet, and in the next few days I had quite a lot of pain in my back and side! This caused great problems as I use my legs to propel the chair backwards. However, my training schedule demands that the nearer you get to a competition, the more training you do. The reason for this is because being in a wheelchair you get stiff quickly. By training four or five times a day you keep loose, but pushing with my feet really hurt my back, so much of the training was counterproductive, since I couldn't get any real speed to race, nor any real power to kick for the field events. By the time the day of the competition came round, I had improved slightly but in no way matched my earlier form or performance. What made it worse was that these were crucial games. Those who did well here would take a giant step towards New York. Praise God it wasn't a disastrous day, in fact, considering the problems it was quite good. As for the Olympics – well, we'd just have to wait and see. At least at this stage there was still a possibility.

Another difficult time was the summer. I've already mentioned the hay fever, but it was a particularly bad year with much discomfort and inconvenience. There are two problems. Having asthma as well, I was never quite sure what I would be suffering from any particular day. If the weather was hot, the pollen count went up, and any medication was only partly successful. If the weather was cold, then you couldn't do anything about it, you can't just swap the drugs around from day to day. That year it was particularly hard to come to terms with, and I wondered how long the season would last, but through the power of Jesus I have learnt to cope. Now I know it is only a limited period, and I believe that, year by year, the problem is being controlled. But again, praise the Lord, although it's an inconvenience, even at its worst, it's never stopped me from doing what I had to do. With these two problems and the fact that I was only slowly using my hand again, I seemed to be making little, if any, progress. However, in spiritual warfare it's not just what is apparent that is important, but what is happening behind the scenes. I was learning a great deal about patience and victory, and perhaps most importantly, about the goodness of God in adversity.

– TWENTY-SEVEN –

The television programme brought renewed interest, and during the autumn I really felt things were beginning to move, and doors open. The new publishers seemed to be interested in the book of poetry, but it would mean quite a heavy financial commitment. I spoke to many friends to see if this was right, and it seemed to be a good idea. The plan was to use some of the money from previous publications and borrow some to make up the difference. By the end of September contracts were signed, and we sat back and waited. There was a great air of excitement. Added to this were new invitations to speak, some unexpected, some were doors I'd been knocking on for a long time. The only disappointment was that no-one wanted "Freedom Ride". There were long delays while the book went to a publisher only to come back rejected, and the whole process would have to be repeated.

I was gradually working my way towards the end of a list. I wasn't sure what was going to happen if there was no response, but I hoped it wouldn't get to that stage. As a result of the broadcast I was approached by Terry Thompson, the director of PHAB (Physically Handicapped and Able Bodied). He had seen the programme and knew of my situation, and had begun to wonder whether there might be a place for me in the organisation where I could exercise a ministry, possibly as a chaplain. He was also concerned, as I was, with the whole question of how the church relates to people with disabilities. Being an organisation aimed at integration in clubs and the wider society, it seemed logical that for Christians integration should also be happening in church. He came to see me, and we had a good time talking about possibilities.

One suggestion was that I might go to the USA to have a look at what was going on there. So by the time Christmas came round, my years in the wilderness seemed to be coming to an end. This was confirmed at new year while I was at the Ranch for a reunion of staff and volunteers. The Lord revealed to me that He was going to do more healing. In fact, on several occasions before this, friends had had visions, pictures, but from this time on they became more frequent, and what I heard the Lord saying was confirmed by two friends who were there. It was 1984, that most famous year written about by George Orwell. For Winston Smith it was a year of fear, but I felt the Lord was going to begin something new for me, and that 1984 was going to be a year to remember.

– TWENTY-EIGHT –

The first piece of good news was that I had passed my exam, which meant that I could go on and do what I hoped would be my last course in the OU. What's more, it was my best grade ever. This year I would be studying popular culture, though already I was beginning to have a few worries about how things would fit together. For the first time, instead of having a few dates and a largely empty calendar, it was reversed. The second piece of good news came a few weeks later, in a phone call from London. It was to invite me to go to America as a team member for Great Britain, to take part in the para-Olympics. I was over the moon about this, and it made the events of the previous July even more special. God had really worked a miracle in spite of the pain. I was excited, although ahead laid arduous preparations, and I wondered how this would fit into my busy schedule. Nevertheless, I felt good. More immediately there was to be a mission in Fulham with the Disabled Christian's Fellowship in early April. Before that there were inoculations, blood tests and endless forms to fill in. Of these, the blood tests were by far the worst. You've heard the expression "getting blood out of a stone". Well, getting blood out of me is very similar, and quite painful! It's not that I object to the needles, but not being able to sit still, it's hard to be accurate. It's enough if I say the bruises were quite marked!

As for the mission itself, I learnt a new lesson. A few days before, I was preaching at St. Paul's in West Bridgford, and everyone remarked on how well I looked. I felt good, and even when I got on the train I was feeling fine. However, by the time the train pulled into St. Pancras there was no doubt I was going down with a cold. Not again, I thought, of all the times . . .! I'd learnt to put up with aching shoulders, aching wrists, asthma and hay fever. After all, although they are inconvenient, you're not actually ill, but I'd already seen the mission timetable, and I knew we'd be very busy. This was definitely not a time to be ill. What's more, it had been suggested that I should do some street work, a new venture for me which I was excited about. But the weather in early April isn't all that reliable – it has been known to snow! Being out in those conditions wouldn't help the cold. That night, the team prayed for me, and you know, although the cold didn't go until practically the last day of the mission, I was never hindered. Although there were times when I felt quite weak and feeble, when it really mattered God gave me energy and clarity of speech. What's more, we were able to go out on the streets and meet lots of people. If anything, the fresh air probably did me more good than harm.

It was an exciting time, being pushed by a friend, just going up to a stranger, introducing ourselves, explaining why we were there. We had some good conversations and were able to tell them about Jesus. There were also amusing incidents – such as the time I got my finger caught in a basket of shoes, and the lady who helped us put the shoes back stayed to talk to us. Then there was the young mother whose child just happened to be called Christian. The most embarrassing moment was in a pub when, having given my testimony, I knocked the table over, drinks included! All in all there were valuable lessons. It doesn't matter what the problem is – God is greater, and even if we're scared stiff of doing something new, if God's told us to do it, it will be good.

– TWENTY-NINE –

After Fulham, time seemed to go by rapidly, and a typical day was as follows: training before breakfast (assuming I got up in time!); training after breakfast, quiet time, study, more training, possibly some relaxation, more training, any preparation, more training, and possibly going out in the evening to speak to a group. I was increasingly away at the weekends, which meant extra training before and after, or if possible a visit to a local park during the weekend. There were also visits to the local study centre to watch OU programmes and of course books to be read and essays to write. I found this a better system than staying up late, or getting up early to watch the broadcasts. That summer holds a record – I actually got through 7 pairs of shoes before the competition, one pair only lasting 6 days! Incidentally, that was the pair I bought from a shop in Fulham! The target date was June 12th. That day we would travel down to Stoke Mandeville, stay overnight, and the following day we would set off for New York. What was even more pleasing to me was that it was the first of two trips I would be making to the USA that year. The second would be in September on behalf of PHAB when I would be the guest of three ministers who either had disabilities themselves or had ministries in that field.

In the meantime there were the Olympic Games. We arrived at Kennedy Airport early evening on Thursday, and were driven out to the Olympic village in special coaches with police escorts. Just to make us feel welcome, we arrived in a rainstorm! Any hopes of being able to settle in and eat were soon dashed – there was lots of red tape to go through first, and it was well into the night before we got to eat and even later before we got to bed. Still, at least we wouldn't be competing until Monday at the earliest, with the opening ceremony on Sunday. I must admit it felt good to be marching around the stadium representing Great Britain and the British team seemed to be quite popular wherever it went. Mind you, it wasn't all plain sailing. I had one or two encounters with the earth at close quarters! I hadn't really thought about the problems of moving around. At home I don't use footrests, as I usually propel myself backwards with my feet. However, over there, there were times when I needed to be pushed, and even a momentary lapse of concentration could prove to be quite painful. One of my worries didn't materialise. It was June, yet I was having no trouble with pollen.

However, heat was a problem, and as you might guess, I got heatstroke on the most important day of the competition! I believe the temperature was in the high 90's that day, so by mid-morning I was already feeling wiped out. My first race had been at 9 o'clock, which meant being in the stadium by 8.30 a.m., but at least it was only 60 metres – the worst was yet to come. At 2 o'clock there would be the 200 metres – I wasn't looking forward to that, and following that would be the kickball and medicine ball thrust, two field events which turned out to be a four and a half hour marathon in the sun, with no shade. It did wonders for my sun tan, but by the time the second competition ended at 7 o'clock, I'd had enough and was feeling slightly disappointed about my performances, However, afterwards I was able to put it into perspective. Not everyone wins a medal, but I had managed to come 7th in both the events. In any case, there were still some surprises to come – on the Sunday I played in the second half of the wheelchair soccer, an exciting game against the USA which we almost turned around. Great Britain won the bronze medal. On the Tuesday I was woken up early to discover I was in the 200 m final. Of course, I came last. In both the world championships and the Olympics I had a 100% record, never winning a race.

However, when you realise that a few years earlier I would not have been able to race at all, and certainly not at this level of competition, then all the glory goes to God for what He has done in my life.

Apart from competitions there was a good social life, and opportunities to share my faith. On one occasion I swam in the Atlantic, but paid for it with quite bad sunburn, though it was enjoyable at the time! There was a trip to New York including a visit to the Empire State Building. Unfortunately we couldn't see much as it rained the whole time. At one point there was even a possibility of a delay going home because of stormy conditions, but late on Sunday night we took off and headed for home.

– THIRTY –

There comes a point where you begin to discern a pattern. I've noticed that, over the last few years. At one time, I'd been fairly trouble-free, my health was good, and circumstances were fairly steady. Now I was beginning to see change. Of course, that didn't mean that I accepted it easily . . . I still wanted those good old days when everything was easy, but during that summer I started to realise that life isn't just blessings and then trials and then blessings, but that the two go together.

If you look at the life of Jesus, there were some who were overjoyed at the Good News, while others completely rejected it. Or you could look at Peter, who at Philippi could say one moment "You are the Messiah",[40] and yet the minute Jesus talked about suffering, came out with "No, that's not going to happen to you, we won't let it". I believe that most of us desire life to go smoothly. We've had our times of testing, it's passed. We've learnt our lesson, now we can get back on an even keel. Yet though I desire that, I have to say that nine times out of ten it doesn't happen. Time and time again when I've thought that it was the end of a particular problem, and it was going to be OK, I discovered that round the corner there's

[40] Mk.8:27-33

another difficulty. I've discovered however that through God's grace we can cope. Furthermore, He is so loving that He allows us to express our feelings. He doesn't condemn us when we say "Oh No, not another . . . Not this . . . not now", but then if we're honest, it's always not now, and just when things are going smoothly, just when you thought it was safe to be a Christian, suddenly another disaster strikes. Our perspective of how big a disaster it is depends directly on the depth of our faith. The more we trust God, the clearer we see the true extent of the problem, and it's a bit like looking at someone through a telescope – they appear to be giant-sized, but when we meet them face to face they are really quite "normal" and not to be feared. It's for this reason that Paul wanted to reassure the Romans[41] that nothing could separate them from the love of God. Some of the things he lists are quite frightening – famine, earthquake, persecution, yet he begins by declaring we are conquerors and that these things can't cut us off from the love of God which is in Christ Jesus. These words have become special to me. They speak of reality, because they speak of the Christian life, the life that Jesus lives. Jesus never said it would be easy, but He did promise that He'd be there[42] and He promised that we too would share in His victory[43].

If in those summer days of 1984 there were lots of good things, there were also lots of disappointments. Arriving back from a trip, I found an article about the publishers of my new poetry book. It turned out they were not all they appeared to be. In fact, the implications were that they cheated people. Further investigations by my friends revealed that there wouldn't be a book, and that it was doubtful if we'd get any money back. There were two things that really upset me. First of all, the money. Apart from what I'd borrowed, the rest was God's money, the proceeds of previous books to be used to proclaim the

 [41] Rom.8:37-39 [42] Mat.28:20 [43] 1 Cor.15:57

love of Jesus through poetry. Secondly, being a writer, I cared about my book. I was excited about the contents and there had already been a long delay. Would it have lost its immediacy even if we managed to produce it, and how could we do that anyway, without finance? To add to this, we still didn't seem to be getting anywhere with "Freedom Ride" – nobody wanted it.

These were the kinds of realities I came back to. America had been good, and in the autumn there would be the return trip. That had been the blessing, but the other side of the coin was that very little else had changed. Add to this the fact that my hay fever came back with a vengeance, and you get a fairly accurate picture of what was going on at the time. I really needed the grace of God that summer.

– THIRTY-ONE –

It came suddenly. I hadn't really had a lot of trouble up to that point. Now, overnight, I found myself wheezy, short of breath. Usually a good sleep will calm down the situation, but not this time. I took my tablets, used my inhaler, but it seemed to be getting worse. By evening I was finding it hard to speak, so you might guess that trying to dictate an essay wasn't easy, but I managed to get it done. Friday was a crucial day as I was packing ready to go off for four or five weeks, and in the evening I was going to see some friends. On Saturday morning I was heading up to Preston for Summer School, but at least by then the situation was more under control with the aid of cough medicine in hot water. It wasn't going to be easy though – Summer Schools are not exactly laid back! The average working day is 9 a.m. to 9 p.m. and that excludes walking back, or in my case riding back, to our accommodation. Another problem was the effort of relating to people who in their turn are not sure how to relate to me, a person with disabilities. By the middle of the week I had managed to make a few friends, which made the second half much better. My respiratory difficulties were now under control, but there were other problems. The most urgent was a puncture, which meant using a different wheelchair for 24 hours. Still, although it was uncomfortable it didn't spoil my two sessions in Blackpool where we were studying cultural activities (popular culture). All in all I survived the week and plunged into the summer activities.

During August we had confirmation that getting our money back from the book would be nothing short of a miracle. I was grateful for friends who prayed about the situation, and cheered me up. Anyway, with the end of summer came the second trip to the states. This was going to be different. For a start the programme was quite heavy. I was going with Mervyn, whom I had met only a few weeks earlier at the PHAB conference, so the early part of the trip would be actually learning about each other, as well as representing PHAB overseas. This was quite a daunting prospect, added to which was the fact that in 8 weeks time there was my exam, so any spare time must be spent in revision. I have to be honest and say that at times, I wondered if I hadn't bitten off too much. Only time would tell.

As we set off for Manchester, I don't think either of us realised just how long a day it was actually going to be. We really appreciated getting into bed nearly 22 hours later! Our hostess the first week was an ordained minister in the Episcopalian church who has cerebral palsy. Though not as severely disabled as I am, she still had a story to tell of resistance to her call. Only after a great deal of patience had she found a place where she was accepted and could exercise her ministry. For much of the first day we shared our common experiences, and over succeeding days we visited several places of interest where sometimes I would talk about PHAB or the church and people with disabilities. Although sleeping in a motel, we spent most of our time in her home where we were made very welcome, and

I think we were quite spoilt. In contrast, the second week was spent in a specially adapted flat in Rochester. Here again, the itinerary was very much the same, and we made lots of friends. The highlight was a brief visit over the border to Canada, to see Niagara, which is a sight I won't forget. Early on the Monday morning we were airborne again, this time for "The Big Apple". In many ways this was perhaps the most difficult, yet most exciting week. It was difficult because for a lot of the time we were left to our own devices, and had to travel mostly on foot and wheel, but at least we saw a great deal of New York, and I had my first taste of a baseball game at the Yankee Stadium.

All too quickly it came to an end and we were preparing to come back to England. It had been a really good time, despite the pressures, and I'd learnt a great deal. I believe I was changed as well, in a way that is difficult to describe but had a lot to do with being even more sure about my call. There were, however, big mountains to climb, not only for myself personally, but for others in a similar position who simply want to participate more fully in the Body of Christ. It would take time. There were many issues to be raised, questions about suffering and healing, about acceptance and participation, but it could be done, not that I ever doubted that, but it's always encouraging to see people fulfil God's purpose for them, despite the obstacles. Eventually there would be a paper which might take things a little further, this would be a report on what I had seen and some suggestions as to how ministry by and for people with disabilities, could be encouraged and enhanced. But before that there was a more pressing need.

– THIRTY-TWO –

All this travelling around hadn't really helped my revision. I had done some work, but not a great deal. However, in just four weeks time I would be taking an exam, hopefully my last in the OU. There were also speaking engagements, but I had to be strict, I wanted to finish without any problems such as resits. When I did get home there was a nice surprise. Two letters from different publishers, asking if I'd considered writing a book! One was from SPCK and one from Marshalls. I replied to both, saying that I had in fact written a book, and would they like to see it? They both maintained their interest, and visits were arranged. The first one was in the middle of revision, the second would be the day after the exam.

The first editor was quite interested, but said it would need extensive re-writing by a professional whom they would try to find. Time flew by, and there always seemed so much to learn, and soon the day of the exam arrived. Still, it wasn't quite as traumatic as the year before when I'd cut my hand, among other things. In spite of advice that I should arrive relaxed and at peace, if I ever needed a miracle now was the appropriate time! Well, I received two, though at first they weren't evident. Indeed, that night I really wondered if I'd have to take a resit. I didn't feel it had gone at all well, but hopefully my continuous assessment would pull me through . . . maybe!

It was in this kind of mood that I met Debbie from Marshalls the following day. I tried to convince her that my next book (this one!) would be the book for them. But after talking for some time, she asked if she could see "Freedom Ride". I said that I had a spare copy that she could look at, and she began to speed read some of it. Then to my utter amazement, she said "We want *this* book!" To say I couldn't believe it would be an understatement, but within two days contracts were drawn up and signed, and preparations were under way. It was exciting to think that the book I never wanted to write and which had taken two years to find a publisher would soon be available for people to read, hopefully to be challenged and encouraged to see what Jesus can do, if we give him freedom in our lives. The most remarkable thing was that the book which was about to be published (apart from one page and a bridging chapter) was the same one that Marshall's had rejected two years before. I mentioned two miracles. The other came on Christmas Eve. My result from the exam. It was a distinction, and early in 1985 I would graduate with a BA from the OU. The years of frustration seemed to be coming to an end. The future was looking good, but then, with God, it always is.

– THIRTY-THREE –

Early in the New Year there was a hopeful sign for the future. I'd been asked to attend a group that was looking into the question of independent living. Its aim was to help people with disabilities to move out into the community. In spite of the setbacks I still cherished the hope that one day I would have my own accommodation, and even though my wrist hadn't fully recovered (I'd discovered most of my injuries take about two years to heal), I'd regained enough abilities to make this a real possibility once more. I'd actually joined a housing association already. Initially the meetings were to investigate all aspects of independent living. These included finance facilities and care. My recent trip to America had shown me just what could be done with the right resources. It was also a chance to meet other people with the same aims. But there were other demands on my time as well. I seemed always to be rushing off somewhere, usually courtesy of British Rail!

In fact, this is another area in which God has been really good, because over the years I've always had a good relationship with those delaing with "Disabled Travel". That's not the whole picture, though. There are problems. Only recently has it become rare to travel in a freezing cold guard's van in midwinter, but perhaps the greatest nightmare is arriving at a station and being left on the train! I have to say that some rail staff still think if you have physical disabilities you haven't got a brain, because of this I do get left on platforms in the cold, or hidden away in a dark office, or worse still, pushed into a corner of the buffet by food and drink that I can't get! On one occasion I spent 4 hours like this on Crewe station, just because they didn't believe I knew which train I needed. It was midwinter, cold and snowing and the journey took about 12 hours, some 5 hours longer than it should have done. Needless to say it was not the most exciting afternoon I have ever spent. Still, praise God, because in the end it doesn't matter how you get there, it's getting there and being used by Him, in the end it always seems to work out. There are miracles. People who have come along at just the right moment to enable me to have a sandwich or cup of tea, or chat. There have even been opportunities to witness. As the months rolled by, the day of publication drew near. It was going to be an exciting time. It was an amazing thought that some people would be reading a book written by me, not because I wanted to receive glory or anything like that, but just that people would be able to read about what Jesus meant to me. After all, this is my greatest ambition, if ambition is the right word to use, because I want every part of my life to speak of His glory and His love for me.

That summer we finally produced "Freedom Song" and after all the problems we'd had, it was still very special to me. It was later in the summer that I was asked by John Pert, specialist Social Worker from the county, to be part of a project to launch people with disabilities into the community. This was a big decision but at the same time it was an honour to be asked, and it seemed the right thing.

So what with OU graduation, all things seemed to be going well, and the best was yet to come.

– THIRTY-FOUR –

It should have been the most exciting time of my life. In three weeks "Freedom Ride" would be published. The build-up had already begun with advertising and yet at that very time I was going through the biggest crisis I'd had so far. There had been signs earlier in the year, slight pains in both my shoulders, tingling in my hands, and a general weakness in my arms, and occasionally very bad headaches, closely connected with my neck. I had gone to the doctor, and I'd been given tablets earlier on in the year, but at that stage it wasn't too much of a problem. When I arrived back at the hostel I realised just how bad it was. I wanted to go to my room, which meant going up in a lift. I've never struggled with lifts, but this time I had great difficulty reaching the button, and when I did reach it I just couldn't push it, there was no power. At first I shrugged it off. It had been cold at Greenbelt, in spite of it being August. I probably just needed to warm up and get the circulation going, but when I tried later on, I still couldn't press the button. In fact, I suddenly realised I had difficulty doing many things. That night I couldn't even get my shirt off. This wasn't the only problem. You will appreciate that being in a wheelchair for most of the day, it has to be comfortable, and obviously one that I can use. When God put me together he decided to give me short legs. This means that because I use my feet to push my chair, I need an especially low one to reach the ground.

Being an active person I tend to get through chairs rather quickly! This has nothing to do with weight (despite what friends say). When I arrived home, I noticed that the chair was in need of a service, but I didn't think it would be a funeral service! The mechanic took one look at the chair and said it was a write-off. I began a saga that wasn't resolved until the end of January. During that time, I tried about 10 chairs, none of which was ideal, or for that matter, even comfortable. Only with the aid of padding and cushions did we finally achieve a temporary solution. Having a chair that isn't comfortable is as bad as having shoes that don't fit. The reality of all this was that I lost mobility and ability, and in spite of waking up each morning and saying that today everything would work out, I was also going to bed saying "well, perhaps tomorrow". It was frustrating, painful, and worst of all, frightening. After all, intitially I didn't know what the problem was. I just couldn't do the things I'd learnt to do. This raised the question of my moving out . . . After all, I had been making progress, moving towards independence. Now I seemed to be going backwards, and there was no clue as to how long this would continue.

The weekend the book was to be published, I was to speak at my church, but even this was put in jeopardy because I came out in a rash and there were fears that this might be something nasty and contagious! Praise God though, we discovered it was just an allergic reaction to tablets. So it was a time of mixed blessings. On the one hand there was all the publicity connected with the book – signing ceremonies and many encouraging comments, and on the other there was frustration and pain, sorrow and joy mixed. Yet I was learning lessons all the time. God sent along some wonderful friends. In addition to the many friends I already had at church, there were Arthur and Caroline. Arthur was studying at St. John's and they were living just across the road from the hostel. It was good to have them around to pray with and encourage me. Towards the end of September I met Ian, who has become a special friend. We were part of a team, brought together by the eveangelist Ian Knox, for a mission in Arnold, Nottingham. We got to know each other really well, so much so that by the end of the day we had already begun to tease each other. Ian's wife Anne is the daughter of the rector of the neighbouring parish of Barton-in-Fabis, whose wife is a physiotherapist. Alastair and Mysie were able to give some advice and some free treatment! I learnt that although I might be down in the dumps, God still loved me. He doesn't change just because we lose our way. When Elijah went into the desert, God was there[44]. He didn't condemn him, in fact He told him to go back, trusting it was all sorted out. All I needed to do was to rest in God and as I did that, He would once again begin to work it out for good!

I don't want to pretend that from that time I felt great – I didn't. There were good days and bad days but even on the worst days there was hope. Gradually I began to settle down, and by the grace of God, cope, because in the end there wasn't any other alternative. God was doing something new. My friends began to notice that most of the spasm that I'd had, had disappeared. My legs were still, my arms weren't jerking, I'd never spoken so clearly, and I could take my own weight. I could even stand up without help. Suddenly lots of things started making sense. Over the past few months many friends had come to share in my healing with words, pictures, dreams, visions. In the midst

 [44] 1 Ki.19:1-18

of the frustration of pain and discomfort there was progress. Slowly I saw that even if one part of my life was a struggle, there were other parts that were blossoming. I couldn't use my hands well for the time being, but I had more control to sit still, stand up and speak clearly. There was another paradox because in the midst of my pain, other people were being healed.

The beginnings of that appeared earlier in the summer. I'd felt for some time the Lord wanted to add some new dimension to the ministry He'd given me. After a workshop on gifts during the mission at Dawlish Warren, I was determined to seek the Lord to see what it might be. It turned out to be healing. I found myself offering to pray for people I was talking to, and finding they were healed. A lady with a disinitegrating spine who two days later was walking about without pain, a friend with headache which disappeared after prayer, and another friend with a badly scalded hand who a day later showed no signs whatever. I was encouraged to go to Sheffield to the "Signs and Wonders" conference led by John Wimber. It was exciting to see the gospel come to life, yet, despite prayer, I came away from the conference still in a wheelchair, and still in pain. I believe some people were puzzled by this, but I'm not. In the end it's God who heals and it's God who is in control of our situation. Whatever I was going through at that time, it was God's will for me. Even if I didn't understand it clearly, and couldn't see the results, God was going to turn it round. Something good would come from it, because that's God's way[45].

[45] Rom.8:28

– THIRTY-FIVE –

In November I had to make a difficult decision. At that stage there were three of us on the project, two of us from the hostel. We had expressed the hope that we would get a house in West Bridgford. Out of the blue we were told we had a house – that was the good news. The bad news was that it was not in West Bridgford. There was no pressure put on us, but a decision would have to be reached in three weeks. The choice was to stay with the project, which would mean losing the area I'd grown to love, or withdrawing, which might mean waiting years for another opportunity. Just when things really seemed to be opening up at my church and in the parish, the whole thing seemed to be up in the air once more. I got in touch with Arthur, Phil and other friends, and asked them to pray. On the Sunday, Arthur drove me round the area to have a look. My first reaction was "Surely God doesn't want me to give up everything and move to a new church where I'd have to start again". It would mean putting off my independence for a while, but in the present situation that might be for the best. But I didn't want to close the door completely. I wanted to hear what God had to say, and doing that was the real turning point. Within a week I knew it was right to go. Several factors became clear. First of all, it wasn't like starting all over again. Even in the Church of England hadn't yet got round to recognising that I had a ministry, the nearest church was St. Andrew's. The vicar turned out to be Reg, a friend from St. John's. From being really not sure, I became absolutely convinced that this was the right thing to do, and by the end of November I knew I would be moving.

All in all, it was a period of adjustment. The book brought new invitations. It also strengthened our case for an appeal for the recognition of the Diocese. I'd settled into a rhythm and there were new experiences ahead – some good, some not. It turned out to be quite a cold winter, and early in the new year I caught a chest infection which was certainly aggravated by cold trains and platforms, and gave me some bad nights. Unfortunate, with so much travelling. There were two trips to Bradford within one week, and then two trips to London again in a very short space of time. My new wheelchair duly arrived at the end of January, and to celebrate the event I travelled north to a recording studio.

Part of the ministries God has given me is to write songs, and over the last couple of years I'd been working with a group of friends called "Contact" from Bradford. Both ministries had decided to produce a tape. Our plan was ambitious. We'd hire the studio for one day, and hoped to complete in that time. I've spent nights in some strange places, but lying on a carpet in a recording studio is probably one of the oddest! Still, after 22 hours the work was done, and within a few days we had the finished product which we were pleased with – their skill and artistry and my writing coming together to glorify God, the body of Christ in action. Speaking of the body of Christ, my work with PHAB had developed to a point where in February of that year we had a day conference with representatives from most of the denominations. As a direct result of this day a steering committee was set up to launch an organisation which could be called Church Action on Disability (CHAD). The time had come to make churches aware of the place for people with disabilities within the Body, and to begin to tackle some of the misconceptions and difficulties that are there.

It was April before the chest infection actually cleared up, and this after very concerted prayer. Nevertheless for the first time for a few months I was feeling good. My shoulder injuries were beginning to heal, and all the time my legs were getting stronger and my speech clearer. It was hoped that my flat would be ready by the Autumn of 1986. By this time the project had changed slightly, in that now there were to be only two people with disabilities in the flats with one tenant carer. I don't want to pretend that every meeting was scintillating. To be honest, there were times when I came out of a two hour meeting and wondered if we'd got anywhere! It soon became apparent that the deadline would not be met. Nevertheless, I believed and trusted that I would eventually be moving out. In the early part of the summer there was really good news. The Diocese had at last come to a decision, and in August while I was in Wales I received a letter from the Bishop of Southwell commending me as one of two lay Diocesan evangelists. What a wonderful day that was; I went with a friend to Barmouth and made several photocopies so I could show people. After 10 years, God had finally opened doors, and the Diocese had given me some recognition.

– THIRTY-SIX –

There haven't really been any more major crises in my life since then, though I have to say as I write this chapter that I still haven't moved into my flat. Autumn 1986 became Easter 1987, and Easter became Autumn. In fact work for a long time seemed to be getting nowhere. At the same time, it's important to see God's hand in this, for even though I am becoming more independent, I do still need a certain amount of care. Although it might be frustrating seeing deadlines passing, it is crucial that everything is right. For instance, work surfaces, doors to get in and out, and emergency procedures in case I get into trouble. I also feel that perhaps the delays have helped me to plan and work out potential problems, to experiment within safety, that God had once again provided the right people. People with the ability to put my ideas into reality.

There are many gadgets in my life now, for instance, a plate on a turntable, and a spoon attached to a lever, with which I can feed myself, an electric razor fixed to a flexible arm so I can shave; a hairbrush sticking out from a wall and a lever which squeezes toothpaste onto a brush. All these are giving me greater independence day by day, and in the flat there will be others. I might even be able to cook meals and make my own drinks. But it isn't just with gadgets that I've improved. I have now taken steps unaided. I've regained nearly all the abilities I'd lost, and after 2 years on tablets for my shoulder, this summer of 1987 in Dawlish Warren (where else?) I came off them and was healed. Another deadline has just passed – the end of October, and of course on one level it's frustrating, but as I approach Christmas, I am aware that very soon I will begin a new chapter, because God is always writing and adding to our story. Just when we think we've reached our climax, He does something new. This summer, it was exciting to see the launch of Church Action on Disability, and within four days the launch of Freedom Ministries, that small group of friends who take care of me, and with their help and support, another chapter has begun. Each new chapter is a testimony to the God who cares, who loves and who turns tragedy to triumph and every sorrow to joy.

– THIRTY-SEVEN –

Over the last few years I've been asked many times to share my understanding of the place of suffering. I suppose it's because of the situation that I'm in and because I'm a Christian. The title of this book is taken from a verse in Romans 8. In that chapter, Paul tackles the subject of suffering. First of all, he declares that the sufferings of this present age are nothing compared to the glory that will be revealed, and then towards the end of the chapter he is convinced that nothing can ever separate us from the love of God. I started this book by saying we can't answer the question "Why?" After 22 years of being a Christian, I still don't know why I have cerebral palsy but I do know what God has done about it. I do know that from a position of hopelessness He has turned my life around. It isn't magic, and you've read enough to know that being a Christian doesn't exempt us from life's problems. There's another comment that I like, this time written by Peter[46]. He says "Why are you surprised at the suffering you're going through?" You see the background assumes that because you're going through bad times it's because you've done something wrong. No one can dispute that part of the pain that we see around us, and in our lives, is because

[46] 1 Pe.4:12 (Author's precis)

of wrong actions and motives. In short, sin. However, there are a whole lot of other areas of suffering that have nothing to do with sin in the personal sense, although they do in a cosmic sense[47]. They have to do with that battle that began way back in time, and in which, whether we like it or not, we are involved. But that battle has been won, and there is a point at which peace will reign in the person of Jesus.

It's all very well being courageous and standing firm, but if I'm going to stand for Jesus I have to know that there is a point to it. Many people would think being a Christian makes my life easier, but in many ways it makes it more difficult, because Jesus demands of me things I would not otherwise want to do. It's some of those activities that bring me into situations of risk and rejection. It's being called as an evangelist that makes me have to travel by train, putting myself in the hands of people who aren't sure how to handle me, and with the best will in the world, I do get some rough rides. Only recently did the inevitable happen on a train jurney. On the way down to Exeter I was dropped out of a taxi onto the pavement, and on the way home, left on a train at Derby and so was two hours late getting home. Sometimes it would be so easy to say I can't be bothered. Alternatively, there are times when I really need to be in full health, because of a busy schedule, when suddenly you are ill . . . That happened last summer when I had a bout of tonsillitis. It happened just as I was starting a very busy six week period with many talks. Now some people would say "Why does God allow you to go through this? Haven't you got enough problems already?" These are fair questions, and to be honest there are times when I've cried out to God "How much more?" But Jesus never said that being a Christian would be easy. In fact it's clear that the reverse is true. He promised that we would have trouble, but he also said we shouldn't be

[47] Eph.6:12

afraid because He had overcome the world. During that bout of tonsillitis He told me quite clearly that He was allowing it to happen because He trusted me. He knew or hoped that I'd still be a witness for Him through the problems and in His power. When I actually took it in, it was a compliment, because Jesus is actually saying "you can represent me".

No, Christianity isn't a crutch for me. Recently I was asked a question. It went like this "If I had the choice between a new body or my Christian faith, which would I choose?" It's a good question. Surely you can understand that given a chance I would gladly run, walk, use my hands and lead a "normal" life, but if I had to do that without Jesus, then the answer would have to be "No". As far as I am concerned, knowing Jesus in my life is worth much more than any new body, because even with the most perfect body there are many people alone, empty and in pain. I would rather continue the life I have with its frustrations, pains, and limitations, but knowing the power of Jesus, than live my life without Him, and anyway, why should I accept second best? One day I'm going to have a new body anyway! There are many situations around us that look hopeless, but God can put them right. All things can work together for good. The key is God. That sentence continues – "for those who love God", and if we are prepared to open ourselves to Him, then He will begin to answer those questions. He will show us the way forward. This isn't a passive surrender, a kind of blind faith. We don't just sit back and say "What will be, will be" because in the same way that God works to turn tragedy to triumph, so He calls us to join Him.

About 2 years ago I was asked to give a talk as part of a concert in aid of Ethiopia. That morning, as I prayed, I was led to a very familiar story. Five thousand people were gathered together to hear Jesus talk[48]. You know the

[48] Mk.6:30-44

rest. What struck me, though, for the first time, were Jesus' words "You yourselves give them something to eat". It started with a small amount of food and ended up with 12 baskets to spare. I understand from that, that if we are prepared to live as God has called us to live, then there will not be starving people, outcasts, the homeless and hopeless. When people cry out "Why doesn't God do something", God points to the cross and says "I have".

There are many areas of suffering that we can confront, challenge and change, and for the rest we must trust God, for He is love. He does care and He sent Jesus to put it right, and there will come a day when we will stand before God, perfect, clean and whole[49]. That is a day that I'm looking forward to, because it's a day when I'll know that all that I've faced has been worthwhile. It's the day when He will say " Well done". It's a day when He will wipe away the tears from my eyes, and those tears are so precious to Him[50]. He's counted every one, kept a record and for those who come through there will be the reward.

He will turn all things for good.

 [49] Rev.21:1-5 [50] Rev.7:9-17

– Epilogue –

All good stories have a fairy tale ending, where the hero or heroine lives happily ever after. The good news is that because of God's grace we will live happily ever after. The bad news is that this isn't a fairy tale. Each one of us would like this story to end with the words, "All is well" but it isn't true and I expect you wouldn't expect it to be so.

Since I wrote the last chapter, three years have elapsed. I moved into my flat in March 1988, and it is great. I enjoy my independence and lifestyle, but it has not been without problems, especially recently. I've had a small fire, an attempted break-in, and an actual burglary. Also there have been other near misses.

One thing that has changed is that I no longer travel as much by British Rail. About two years ago, Freedom Ministries who supports our work, agreed that I could have assistance. Philip was the first to join us, he comes from Nuneaton. This has given us much more freedom, as I now travel the country in a little red Astra.

Phil and I have spent a great deal of time together. One person recently pointed out that we probably spend more time together than the average married couple. He is a great asset, but even here there are problems. In March 1991 he injured his back, which for him was painful, and for us both could have been a major problem. However, God stepped in, and through his disability, I have gained more independence than I've ever had before.

More recently Jonathon has joined us full time, and others have volunteered to join a reserve team.

As for other things, I'm still involved with CHAD and PHAB and still make occasional comebacks in sport! Also, I'm still writing. I'm about to release my tenth book of poetry, and there are other books in the pipeline.

I believe that God still has a lot to do in my life, including taking me out of this chair. Some of the things he does will be easy, and others will be hard, but I know that whatever he does, or asks me to go through, is because he loves me and wants the best for my life. He loves you too, and if you will trust Him, he will turn all things for good.